I Chose The Eagle

Thanks for coming. It was wonderful seeing you again

Pat

ISBN: 978-1-952485-98-5

Redhawk Publications
The Catawba Valley Community College Press
2550 US Hwy 70 SE
Hickory NC 28602

I Chose The Eagle

A Lifetime with Friends in Art and Travel

Patricia Wreyford Viles

This book is dedicated to

Miss Lerah Emerson

Teacher Extraordinaire

who taught me to fly and

whose spirit is always with me.

And to my beautiful friend and fellow artist,

Mona "Vae Cunningham" Hamilton

who left us October 3, 2022.

Rest in Peace, my friend.

We will meet again.

"Festival Day in Hickory," North Carolina, the town where I live. French dyes on silk.

TABLE OF CONTENTS

Huge crane in the park. Watercolor by Patricia Wreyford Viles

INTRODUCTION

This book is about the choices we make that affect our lives. It is about stretching our wings. It is about getting outside our box. It is about following our star. It is the story about how I became a world traveler after going back to college at age 42 and studying French for three years, learning to read, write, and speak that beautiful language, eventually becoming fluent enough to do that. This gave me a tool I needed to take on the world. When you learn one language other than your natural one, it is easier to learn others well enough to get along. It is about painting in Europe, Asia, all over the USA, and since my husband traveled a lot for business, I was able to go to other countries like South and Central America, Canada, Mexico, Norway, Denmark, Sweden, and other destinations. I was not alone all the time. My husband went to many of those places with me when he could. I was not always alone when he couldn't go. I went on to painting workshops with professional artists and friends.

During those trips I met many people who helped me learn to be more tolerant, handle difficult situations, know that I could travel alone and be safe and happy, and make friends that would last a lifetime. It has been an enchanted life.

Now that I am living in the age of cell phones and GPS, I shudder at the memory of going to foreign countries alone, buying a map, renting a car, spend weeks and sometimes months, either traveling to paint or going to language school. Would I do it again? You bet. My hope is that those who read these pages will learn something that will enhance their life, broaden their horizons and help them understand they have choices. Not everyone will have the chances I have had, but there is a big wide world out there and lots of places to explore. Take advantage of it. Now, this doesn't mean that I didn't take advantage of all the wonderful places we have in the USA. With my husband's business travels, I went with him a lot after the children were away from home, and sometimes they would go with us during the summers.

Becoming an artist was not a choice for me. It was a gift. When my children were small and I was a full-time mother, my husband noticed I liked to draw and paint with the children. For my birthday he gave me a set of acrylic paints, some canvas boards, paint brushes and a book on how to paint. Within a week I had copied all the pictures in the instruction book, and then graduated to pictures in other books and magazines. It didn't occur to me that I could go outside and paint what I saw or make a flower arrangement and paint it or use photographs I had made until a year later. When I finally realized I could do that, my world opened, and I became more aware of my surroundings. So, while the children and their friends played, I painted. It was wonderful.

Years later, when the children were older, I took my first painting workshop with a local artist, and once again my world opened. Not long after that, my husband took another job, and we moved to Hickory, North Carolina. After settling in, getting the kids in school, and the house in order, I became a member of a small group of artists and joined the local museum.

One day while shopping, I saw an *American Art* magazine on the newsstand, put it in my shopping cart, and finished my shopping. As soon as the groceries were put away, I made a cup of tea and sat down to read the magazine. In it was an article about an artist from St. Louis, Missouri, James Godwin Scott, who would be teaching a watercolor workshop in Sault St. Marie, Canada. Whoopee. An adventure... My husband Art, and I talked about this, and he said, "Go." I went. Not only was this a wonderful trip to paint and learn, but it would be in a country I had never visited. Jim and his workshop attendees became good friends. After painting with Jim and his group of artists, I was on fire. I took many workshops with him and his followers over the years, and he became like a member of my family.

Some of the workshops I attended with Jim was to the American Southwest, and I fell in love with that area, the people and the history of the Four Corners region. To this day I am passionate about pictographs, petroglyphs, all the ancient Indian Ruins, and the Native Americans. I never tire of looking at the glyph sites and find myself making up stories to fit the ones I see. From the ones I see on the road between Velarde and San Juan Pueblo, to the incredible sight in Horseshoe Canyon, I have hiked, photographed, and enjoyed the history of the great American Southwest. The feelings I have when I stand before the panels dating back to 6500 BCE are wonderful. How could they have done such beautiful work with the limited tools they had? How could these works have survived so many centuries? The carvings are simple but to me are very sophisticated.

After 30 years of plein air painting throughout Europe, Asia, the United States, South and Central America, I have become a studio painter, but I know without a doubt I would never be able to do what I do today without the years of working on location. Being a globetrotter prepared me to become much more open to change, gave me extended families throughout North, South, and Central America, France, Spain, the Caribbean Islands, and England, and other countries in Europe. I have five passports covering all the years of traveling. All the traveling prepared me to become a globetrotter and, hopefully, a more accomplished artist. You can't get that from a book.

ACKNOWLEDGEMENTS

Writing this book has brought back memories covering 30 years of travel in several European countries, Central and South America, Canada, many Caribbean Islands, and Asia, as well as many states in America to paint and study art. Knowing another language made it possible to travel outside the United States and also made it easier to learn other languages as well.

The people written about in this book are all real, and it is the meeting of them and the experiences we shared that sustain me now that I no longer travel! Having these memories made it easier to write this book. I owe a debt of gratitude to everyone who helped me remember details of the trips we made together, the camaraderie we shared, and the friendship we still share.

Huge thanks go to my family and friends for understanding my need to take on this project and for helping me make it happen. Without them, this book would never have been possible! Enjoy!

PREFACE - 1953

She sat there, in an overstuffed chair, wearing a blue dress with white lace collar and cuffs, resembling a lady from another century. She matched the room perfectly: Large scaled Victorian furniture, tasseled lampshades, dim light, and antimacassars she had crocheted on the arms of the sofa and chairs. A busy Persian rug completed the décor. I loved her very much, this special teacher.

We washed and set each other's hair as we had so many times before, and while we waited for it to dry, we talked about school and the subjects I would take in high school the next year. She made us tea, and we continued our conversation.

Suddenly, she turned toward me, and with tears in her eyes, said, "My dear child, I have something to tell you." I was afraid. The look on her face told me something was very wrong. I looked at her and realized she was very pale and had lost weight.

"My dear child," she said again, "I have something to tell you. You know I have not been teaching lately, and there is a reason for that. I have been sick and in the hospital for a while. I have an illness named Leukemia and there is nothing more the doctors can do for me. This means I will die soon. I tell you this because I don't want you to hear it from someone else. Knowing you has been a privilege! You are the daughter I never had, and I thank God for you."

By then I was sobbing, and she came to sit beside me on the sofa. She put her arms around me and began speaking again. "I want you to know how special you always have been to me. I want you to know you have a fine mind. I know your family's economic situation and it will be difficult for you to get an education, but you must and you will find a way."

"My dear child, you have a choice to make!" With her small right hand on the arm of the sofa, she walked her fingers forward, and said, "You can crawl on your belly like a worm and see only what is in front of you," and then, waving her arms in the air, said , "or you can soar like an Eagle and see the world." I understood! I made a vow to her that I would.

Miss Lerah Emerson passed away a few weeks later. Then, I dusted off my wings and flew.

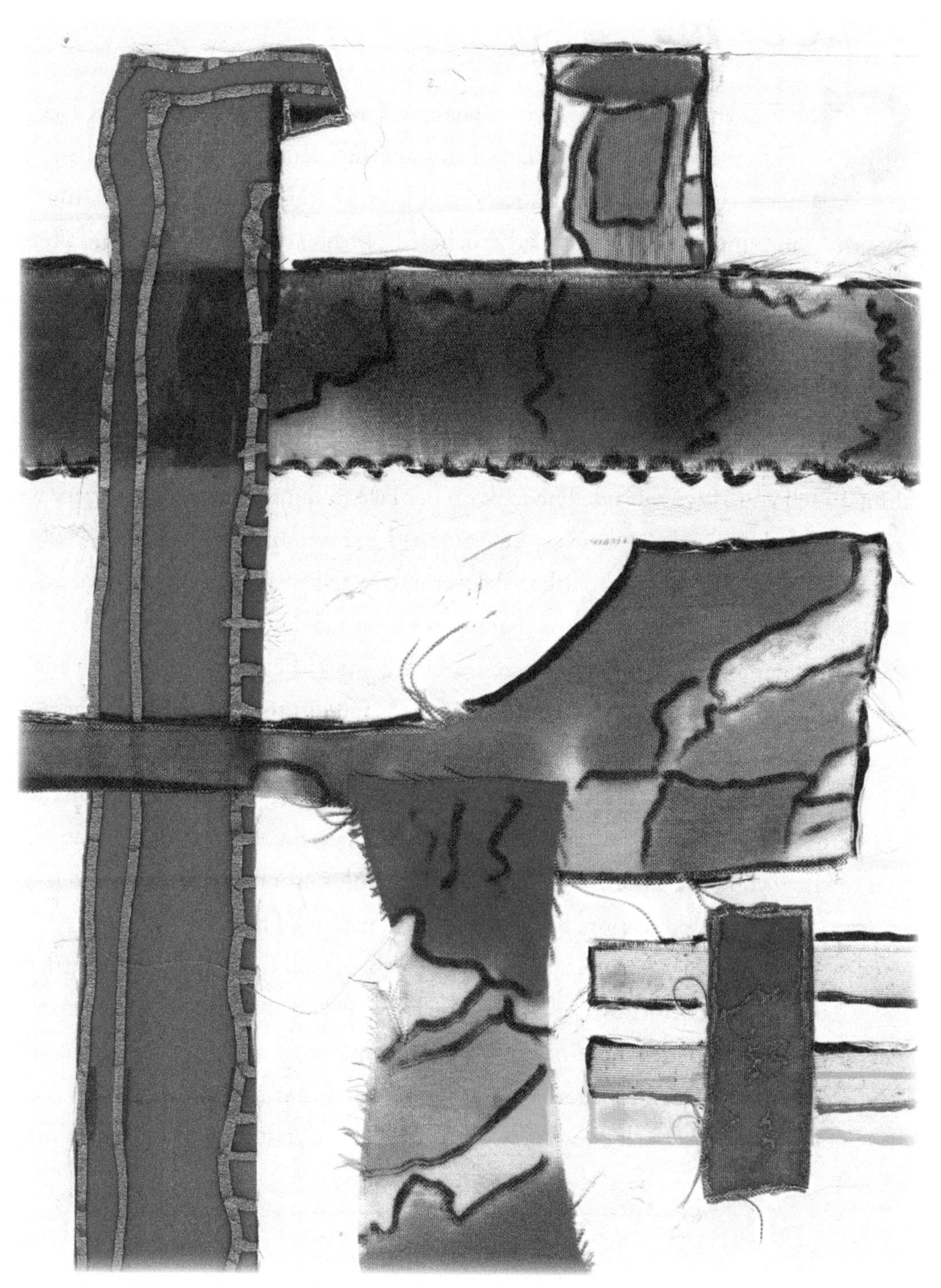

"Pathways." Small painting made with hand-painted silk scraps.

MEMORIES

Where do I begin to tell the story of a life so full of wonderful happenings, fantastic memories, and so many trips to exotic places most people never dream about? Too much time has passed to remember the day-to-day happenings of my youth. Even memories of high school have faded into oblivion, and the early years of marriage, adopting children, and being the wife of a corporate executive have all faded with time.

My life really changed after the children were grown and away from home, going to college, living their own lives. It was only then that I began traveling to paint, learn another language, and became a citizen of the world, particularly France. Even some of those memories go so far back they are like an old movie that has been played over and over so often they have become faded, skipping sections of conversations and not making much sense. But it only takes a word or seeing a photo to bring back memories of a friendly face; to bring back those cherished times.

My fascination with people of other countries began when my children were teenagers. I read an article in our local newspaper about a program that was bringing teenagers from other countries to live with American families for six weeks during the summer, to learn English and our way of life. There was also another program that brought French teachers of English to America to better learn English and more about our way of life. They were to live with American families and participate in our daily lives. We decided to host a teacher, applied, and were sent information on Madame Nicole Morange. Madame Morange lived in the small town of Panazol, a suburb of Limoges, France. Nicole was an English teacher at a girl's school in her town. Her English was perfect but was spoken with a British accent! My kids were fascinated with her. She joined us that summer for 6 weeks, and we had a wonderful time together! Adventure with these people are written about in another chapter!

Nicole was excited about her visit with us and was happy to do anything that would broaden her view of America, our people, and our way of life. She was happy to do anything to accomplish her goal. We took her on trips to our mountains, our small house on Seabrook Island, South Carolina, museums, our Protestant church (she was Catholic), visited family and many friends. We all had a wonderful time getting to know each other, and my kids had a good lesson in learning about people from another country.

The next summer, we had another teacher: Jacqueline Bans and her husband Jacque! They lived in a suburb of Paris: Mante-la-Jolie. Jacqueline's English was good, but her husband only spoke French and a bit of Spanish. I had not yet gone back to school to learn French but had a wonderful time talking with Jacque anyway, learning quite a lot of their beautiful language in the process! Jacque was also a teacher in the same school as Jacqueline. The six weeks these interesting people were here passed quickly, and our family was sad to see them leave. I promised to visit them as soon as I could and did go there several times during the following years. Because of these two couples, I eventually studied French at Lenoir-Rhyne University and became good at it: not completely fluent, but close.

While Jacque and Jacqueline were here, we took them to one of our local restaurants, Mom and Pop's Fish Camp located in a small town close by. The food there was good and always fresh. I explained the menu to Jacqueline, and she interpreted for Jacque. I tried to help him decide what he would like to have for dinner, and the conversation went something like this:

I said to Jacque, "Jacque, the fish platter is large and has a lot of food on it. It might be better if you chose a regular plate." Jacqueline translated and he said, "Je suis tres faim," and patted his stomach. That meant he was very hungry and would like the larger portion. When his platter was placed in front of him, his eyes got huge. The platter was running over with fried fish, French fries, slaw, and bread! He was a good sport and did a decent job of eating the food. At the end of the meal, the waitress saw the excess on his plate and asked if he wanted a doggy bag! I explained what that meant to Jacqueline, and she translated for Jacque. His reply was: "My dog lives in France and the food would be spoiled before I go home!" This, of course, was in French but I had picked up enough of the language by then to know what he had said. When I told the family, they and all the other restaurant patrons near us were laughing.

By the way, we all turned down dessert!

For the next several years we hosted teenagers. They were from different European countries. Usually there were two each summer, but one year we decided on four, and had a French boy and girl and a Spanish boy and girl. Their names were Muriel Chenebault, Stephane Morange, Sophie Huet de Guerville, and Bu Lorenza. It was like a little United Nations around here! Those kids were simply fantastic and my kids, Eric and Janelle, were fascinated with them. Our house was alive with music, three languages, neighborhood kids, kids from our church, and others who learned of our visitors. Our swimming pool was constantly filled with them, and it was like a three- ring circus around here the entire summer and we loved it!

A trip to Disney World was the highlight, and all six kids had the time of their lives. I think they rode every ride there, engaged in every available activity, ate tons of junk food and got excellent tans! They were a joy to be with and we were all sad when they had to leave. This summer activity went on for many years until I learned about a new way of teaching French at our local university.

For the first semester, I would get six hours credit by attending the master class, an hour in conversation class and another hour in the laboratory. We were not allowed to speak English while on campus, and that sounded like it would be interesting, so I decided to go there and learn French. In a later chapter you will read about my nearly three years of studying languages and becoming pretty darn good with French!

I am still in touch with most of the young people who were here. My husband and I attended many weddings of these kids, christenings of their children, entertained their parents when they came to visit, met some of the parents in New York City for a week of attending stage shows, and going to other interesting places.

Having these people as friends and visiting them in their homes was one of the reasons why I went back to college to learn French! That language opened the world to me. Knowing French made it much easier to learn Spanish and Italian, but I never became accomplished enough to be able to carry on a complicated conversation in those two languages! However, it was difficult for the Europeans to understand my kids English, since it was spoken with a distinct Southern accent, so I had to work hard to change that! There was much laughter among all of us when it came to communication!

I had a difficult time with the French pronunciation until I went to school in Paris, Avignon, and Aix en Provence in France, and also a special course in conversation at Dartmouth College in Hanover, New Hampshire. Other visitors we had were from were from various parts of Europe. Chantel Fouquet, (France), Gladys Felix (Spain), Ersula Keller, (Germany), Michaela Capra, (Spain), Ali Mesfoui, (Morroco), Khalid Mirano, (Morroco). We learned as much from these interesting people as they did from us!

One late Fall and early Winter, my husband and I went to Costa Rica on a building team mission with our Methodist Church. We spent nearly three months there working on an addition to the small community church. This addition was to be housing for the young pastor and his family. There we became acquainted with several church members, who worked with us building the new home.

After we returned home from Costa Rica, we talked with our family and decided to invite the pastor and family, and several of the older children to spend Christmas with us. This was possible since their school season was completely different than ours and their summer vacation was during our winter! We made arrangements for their flight, met them at the airport, and for the next six weeks our house was a rollicking, loud, and very busy place and much fun was had by all. By then our own kids were away in college and missed all the fun!

These wonderful people were the last to spend time with us for a while. This was about the time I began learning French at Lenoir-Rhyne College, now a University. The school had implemented a new immersion study of French, and I decided to enroll in the French classes. My husband and I were still meeting French friends in New York and sometimes in the Southwest, but the three years of my study kept me at home and busy!

Having these special kids from France and Spain was exceptionally good for our local teenagers and younger kids. Kids of our friends were always included in our activities, so they became fast friends and some of our local young people traveled to either France or Spain to visit the families of the kids who had been here with us.

But after several years, I knew if I wanted to become a real artist, my art had to be my main focus. After that, my travelling was dedicated to painting on my own, and later, different friends would join me. Those were wonderful years. We had lots of fun, did a tremendous amount of work, and I began exhibiting my paintings all over Europe and Asia. My experiences in Europe and Asia are told in another chapter.

Years passed, and now I do not travel much, but I still paint every day and write a lot! Life goes on!

THE BEGINNING

On October 17, 1938, a baby girl was born at 2 am in Fordyce, Arkansas to Bernice Sybil Turner Wreyford and Burlon O'Dell Wreyford.

That baby was me! They named me Patricia Gale, later changed to Gail! My mom said I was born squealing at the top of my lungs and yelling, "Let me do it myself." According to her, I was the most independent child ever born and I remain that way 'til this day. I suppose the spelling of my middle name was prophetic! My younger brother, Samuel O'Dell, was born in 1941 and a year later my sister Martha. We adopted Constance Louise, calling her Connie, and spoiled her very much.

It has been eight decades since I was born in Arkansas, and those years have passed very quickly. Sometimes, when I am trying to remember things that happened so long ago, I find it very difficult to bring up an accurate picture.

Both the Turner and Wreyford families lived in the area around Fordyce and other towns close by. I enjoyed visiting my Aunt Thalia and playing in her beautiful flower garden. She had the most beautiful dahlias ever, and everything she touched turned out beautiful. Aunt Thalia was well known for her flower garden and the gorgeous quilts she made. Aunt Gertha lived close by too and she played the piano like a professional. These ladies were my father's sisters and they lived in Waldo, Arkansas.

My mother's sisters, Aunt Ada, Aunt Bertha, and Aunt Hazel lived not too far from us and I remember many happy times playing with their children.

When I was about 4 years old, my Dad got a job in Oak Ridge, Tennessee, with Rust Engineering, working on a project he could not talk about. That's when we were all packed into a car and were taken to Oak Ridge to live, seldom seeing family again. We had a few trips back to Arkansas by train but not often.

We were living in a part of Oak Ridge where a lot of the workers on the project were located. Since my brother, sister, and I were young, we did not go to school, and I had no one to play with during the day. One day, early in the morning, I was outside and saw some children walking to school with a lady. I was crying loudly! The lady stopped and said, "Why are you crying? Are you ok?"

I said, "I have no one to play with! I want to go to school too." By then my mom had come outside, introduced herself to the lady, and they had a short conversation. Then the nice lady said to her, "I walk by here every day. Would you let Patsy go to school with us? She can amuse herself and then play with the children during recess and lunch." My mom agreed and went into the house and packed my lunch.

It was wonderful! I played all morning with the toys and coloring books. When the teacher asked the children to come to the reading circle, I went too. She handed out the book, and I said, "I want to read too!" She gave me a book, and I read it out loud! Before that day, no one knew I could read!

So that day, in a very small school with few children in the class, my love of books and learning began and continues to this day!

I remember one year when I was about six, we were visiting our families in Arkansas during the Christmas holidays, and Santa Claus came to see us while there. We were staying with Aunt Hazel. I don't remember much about her house, but I think it was white with a white picket fence around it. I had gotten a baby doll from Santa and loved her very much. One morning I looked for my baby doll and she was not to be found! I looked everywhere: Under the bed, under chairs, sofa, any place I could think of, and she was not there! I cried until I was hiccupping! Aunt Hazel asked,"Did you leave your baby outside?" I did not think so but went to look anyway. I found her stuffed between the slates of the fence, her head cracked, and she was wet. It had rained during the night. I screamed, brought everyone running and discovered that my cousin Royce, had put the doll there. I hated Royce! I wished he would die! My doll was ruined! My parents could not afford another doll. Royce got a spanking, and Aunt Hazel took some of her grocery money and bought me another doll.

I loved Aunt Hazel for the rest of her life! The new doll eventually went to dolly heaven and I never thought of her again, but my memory of what my aunt did stayed with me through the decades, even after she passed away. I also learned a valuable lesson from that experience and that was to be careful what you do, or you could make problems for someone else. I know that now Aunt Hazel could not afford to replace my doll at that time and neither could my parents, but she did anyway. And, yes, Royce got a spanking and apologized, both to his parents and to me.

Another memory I have of those younger years was a visit to the same family. I was about eight. My cousin Royce and I were playing together. We decided to see who could run around the house the fastest. I went one way and Royce the opposite. We met at a corner, slammed into each other and both of us broke our collarbones! Out of all my cousins, Royce is the only one I remember best. We were the same age. After that trip, I hardly ever went back "home" again. My dad was always working, and it was hard for my mom to travel on the train with three small children. There was never enough money for traveling anyway. And we begin moving around a lot after that.

When I was in the 6th grade, we moved to the tiny community of Blowing Springs, a few miles from Clinton, Tennessee. It was way out in the country. Our house was on the hill and I used to begin at the top of the hill and turn cartwheels all the way to the road. That's as close as I ever got to being an Olympic champion!

It was very friendly and community in spite of the houses being so far apart. On Halloween night several neighborhood children would meet at a prearranged place and go from house to house trick or treating. All the neighbors had candy for us or special treats of some kind so there was no tricking. Daddy would have been upset if we had done any damage to our neighbors' houses!

Sometimes, during the harvest season, mom would work some, but she always had something for us to snack on when we got home from school. One day we came in and found a beautiful banana cream cake on the counter top. My brother, sister, and I proceeded to eat most of it! When mom came home she was very upset that we had eaten the cake she prepared to take to church that night, and there was no time to make another. To make matters worse, there were three very sick children that night, and we didn't get to go to church! I cannot eat a banana or anything with banana in it!

After a period of time we moved to another town in Tennessee named Woodbury. We lived in a two-level house situated on the main highway to town. Across the road was a family with children our age that we played with a lot. It was while living there that we finally got a dog, a beautiful collie we named Golden Sun and called him Sunny Boy. In the afternoon after school Sunny would walk us across the road, then lie at the end of our walk, waiting to bring us home in time before supper. Sunny took good care us.

Just before we had moved there, we had adopted our new infant sister, Connie, named Constance Louise. During the day, mom would put her in a playpen on the front porch and Sunny would lie between her and the walk, and no one who was not family or friend could get close to the playpen! Sunny really took good care of us!

One afternoon, after taking us across the road to play, Sunny was laying at our walk waiting to bring us back home, minding his own business. We had a neighbor about a mile down the road who had a large cattle farm. He had tried several times to buy Sunny to train him to work his cattle. Not so long after taking us across the road, the neighbor was driving toward town, saw Sunny lying there, several feet from the road. The idiot deliberately crossed the highway and ran over Sunny killing him instantly! We saw this happen and became hysterical. Our Daddy dug a grave and buried Sunny behind the house, having a special service for Sunny. Every kid in the neighbor was devastated! I don't remember what happened to the man. I hope he rots in Hell now! It was a long time before we got another dog.

During the next several years, Dad's work took us too many different places. Each year, I went to two or more different schools until we finally moved back to Clinton when I was a high school freshman. We lived in a very small house on a high hill. Every day we would walk to school along the railroad tracks. Most of the kids who lived on the hill walked together. It was in Clinton that I finally got to stay in school until I graduated from high school in 1965 with a scholarship that I used to go to business school in Knoxville, a large city about 25 miles from Clinton. My Mom drove me to Knoxville every day and waited until I finished classes to go home.

I believe all the moving around we did when I was young prepared me to be able to make friends fast and leave them without grieving. Each move was an adventure and helped me to grow up to be very independent and to take advantage of new situations.

After finishing business school, I got a job at Dunn & Bradstreet in Knoxville working as a file clerk. Most people thought it would be a boring, nothing of a job, but for me, it was fascinating! I learned more about East Tennessee and Western North Carolina, the cities and counties in those areas, the business, how people lived, worked, played, etc., and to this day, I can still recall the names of the county seats, the capitals, the diverse small communities, and know instinctively where they are located.

Getting to work was a problem, but I began riding the bus every day and got to know the regulars. One day the bus was crowded. The only seat available was in the back next to a handsome young man. I recognized him from high school! He had graduated two years before me and was attending college at the University of Tennessee. He had been riding with a friend but the friend's car was out of service, so they had to ride the bus. His name was Ardle Lee Viles. Six months later we were married!

And so another chapter in my life began. And what a chapter it was!

GETTING OUT OF MY BOX

I think in a way, we all live in a box of our own making, from the time we are born until we get old enough to realize we are limiting ourselves. When we begin to realize there is much more "out there," and we are willing to spread our wings, the world is waiting for us and it may seem scary at first, but is it?

When I was a child, my family was frequently moving from one town or state to another in order to make a living. By the time I graduated from high school, I had attended several different schools. I was lucky to attend the same high school all four years. Situations like this can make or break a child. I had to learn fast how to make friends and how to let go of them when we moved on. I had to learn how to cope with many different situations: When to be quiet, when to speak up, accept people as they were, and not make judgments. There was no way to stay inside a box if I didn't want to be lonely.

So, I made friends fast and gave them up when necessary. The upside of this is that no matter where I go, I can fit in. I can go to France, Spain, England, Japan, or Korea and fit in. I can go anywhere in the world I want to go and make friends and these situations are not scary. However, to be able to do that requires one to be open; in their thinking, always aware of what is happening around them, and have the desire to learn about others from different cultures and of life. Our expectations must not be too outrageous. Of course, learning to speak, read, and write French gave me an advantage in all French speaking countries, and made it easier to pick up other languages like Spanish and Italian good enough to not starve or get lost. Also, people from different countries appreciated my efforts to communicate with them in their language.

But in countries like Japan, Korea, Greece, etc., where the languages are so different, I was dead in the water. No matter how hard I tried, I could only pick up a few phrases like "Where is the ladies' room?" or "How far is the museum?" and they were forgotten as soon as I got on the plane to come home. I had to become an actress, acting out my needs with gestures or depend on others for help. I was lucky to have my friend Kichung Lee Lizee with me in Japan and Korea. Kichung is Korean-American and speaks Japanese and Korean as well as being fluent in English. Alone, I would have been like a lost ball in high weeds. Thank you, Kichung. You kept me out of trouble and made the trips wonderful.

There were many things I did to prepare me to get out of my box and one of the first was to go back to college and study languages. That experience is written about in its own chapter, "Learning French." Getting an introduction to Spanish and some private lessons in Italian opened the world to me, and I am grateful to have had the opportunity to do those things and a husband who understood my desire to "stretch my wings."

One of the most interesting things about getting out of my box was and still is: ART. No matter where I went there would always be several people who would stop to watch me paint. They would get excited recognizing what I was painting, chattering away, and if I was in France, I kept quiet to hear their opinion. Sometimes it was difficult to keep a straight face. The French people love art. Knowing another language was instrumental in my being able to make new friends that I have stayed in touch with for many years. I found that art brings people together in a special way in most of the countries I have visited as well as in my own country of the United States of America.

For many years, before I began traveling to paint, I painted most of the time in my backyard or in the forest where my home is located. The woods were full of forest creatures who regularly came to snatch the food I put out for the feral cats, birds, racoons, squirrels, chipmunks, etc., and I took pictures of them. There is always something interesting, funny, and once in a while serious happening. For instance, one late afternoon I had put out several small bowls of food for the evening meal. That particular afternoon a mother racoon brought her three babies with her. They were old enough to eat the cat food I had put out for all the animals. The babies ate a little of the food then one of them went to the bucket of water, climbed on to the rim and began drinking. The other two babies followed suit, climbed on to the rim, dislodging the one already there. He fell head first into the bucket. Mama continued eating, the baby could not get out of the bucket, and the two on the rim just kept drinking. I grabbed a towel, ran out, pulled the baby out of the bucket, shook him a bit then wrapped him in the towel, drying him as good as I could. Mama finally came over. She began licking the baby, then wrapped herself with her baby in her mouth, around my legs. I guess that was her way of thanking me for saving her baby. The last museum exhibit I had I painted a series of nine watercolor paintings of these adorable forest creatures. The paintings were all the same size and format. That series now resides in the home of a Virginia family. It would have been easy to stay comfortable in my studio where everything I need is at hand but there is a lot to be said for painting outside.

I have to admit my studio is usually messy, but I know what is in each pile on the table and I do manage to keep a nice, clean area where I can work when the mood hits. What fun it was to search through the piles of paper and other stuff, finding many things that could be used in a collage. There would always be something special hiding in one of those piles that could make a collage painting better. Piles of papers, fabrics, pictures from magazines, bottles and tubes of paint in different mediums, etc., are fun to search through, especially when I am working on a collage. It is exciting to search through different piles of "stuff" and have an "aha" moment that sends me off on a different tangent or thought that changes the entire feeling of a painting. And it is necessary to have all the different mediums I use close by. Fortunately, I have two nice size closets with shelving in which I can store supplies.

One afternoon, my friend Joann Wilfong dropped by for a visit while I was cleaning off my studio work table, going through scraps of silk fabric I had painted and throwing away some of them. Joann asked, "Why don't I take this trash away? My trash collector comes tomorrow morning, and your wastebasket is nearly full." I agreed. We visited for a while then went to the kitchen to have tea and cookies. I thought she was acting a bit strange. She had never been in such a hurry to leave. She called the next morning and said she was coming over. I hurriedly cleaned up the studio a bit in case she wanted to paint.

When she came in she had a grocery bag full of the silk scraps she had taken home with here the day before, and a handful of small mats she had cut. She began laying the silk out on the table and placing the mats on certain areas. ¡Voila! There were small paintings from the scraps I had thrown away the day before. We were both so excited we were throwing silk all over the table, laying mats on certain areas, finding more small paintings. Finally, we settled down, got serious about what we were doing. Soon we had the possibility of 39 small paintings. While Joann began matching the mats and frames, she had brought, I ironed the silk so we could frame them. After we had used up all the supplies we had on hand, Joann went shopping for more mat board and frames. When the job was finished, we decided to donate the paintings to the Museum gift shop. There are still a few of the little paintings remaining there.

It was good to have supplies on hand for emergencies or when an accident occurs. For instance, one evening I got ready to go to a formal event at the art museum. I had a few minutes before I had to leave so I went into the studio and began working on a small painting. Whoops. I got paint on my formal black dress I had made for the special occasion. Not to worry. I took the dress off and using textile medium mixed with acrylic liquid paint that dries very fast, painted on a design, then went to the party. Several ladies asked me where I got the dress and I told them I made it and it was one of a kind. Everywhere I go I look for bits and pieces of things I might could use in my art. In order to be a collagist or mixed media painter you must be a packrat. I am aways bumping into things and have pockets full of "stuff." Bruises are normal on a packrat.

At this point, I must let you in on a little secret. I don't consider myself a real artist. I don't have a website, I don't teach workshops and I don't have reproductions made of my paintings. I don't enter competitions. What I do is have fun. Every time I go into my chaotic studio, I am transported into another world. A world of color, line, shape, form, and imagination. I become like a kid again. I get out of my box. And that, to me my friends, is what making art is all about.

However, painting is not all I do in my studio. My computer is also there. But until I began writing this book, I seldom used the computer, preferring to write letters by hand. I try very hard to keep up a correspondence with my friends from other states and countries, but I must admit the truth: I have not been diligent in corresponding with them the way I should, and I do regret that. But, they have been quiet also. Recently, I made a promise to myself that I will try harder to get in touch with them, catch up with their family happenings, and let them know how things are with me. I will try to be a better friend to them and my local contacts. Who knows? I may be on a plane going somewhere before long.

Till a voice, as bad as conscience
rang interminable changes

On one everlasting Whisper, Day and
Night repeated…So:

"Something hidden. Go and find it.
Go and look beyond the Ranges---

"Something lost behind the Ranges. Lost
And waiting for you. Go."

—Rudyard Kipling's "The Explorer," 1898

If a man does not keep pace with his companions, perhaps it is because he hears a different drummer.

Let him step to the music he hears, however measured and far away.
—Henry David Thoreau

LESSONS I HAVE LEARNED IN LIFE

Trust in God

Be Patient

Do Not Withdraw Emotionally

Detach Myself from the Problem Not the Person

Depend on Myself but Ask for Help When I Need it

Trust Myself

Love Myself

I Can Do Anything If I Try Hard Enough

Share With Others and Get Lots in Return

Learn Something New Every Day

Make Friends and Keep Them By Being a Friend

Love Unconditionally

Never Be Judgmental

Be Passionate

Have No Fear of the Unknown

When You Change the Way You Look at Things, The Things You Look at Change

Always Embrace Change

Expect Everything and Be Prepared to Deal with Disappointment If I Don't Get It

Don't Gossip

Paint Everyday Possible for That Keeps Me Sane

Be Thankful for Everything I Have and Thankful for the Things I Don't Have

Neil and the boys!

Red Dog and Spencer with Nancy.

THREE BLESSINGS

One morning early the phone rang. The caller, was Sharon, a friend of my sister Connie. Sharon was a volunteer with the local Humane Society. We chatted a few minutes, then she said she had a question. Someone had called the Society and said there was a very nice dog that had been seen running loose through their neighborhood: a full blooded Shetland Sheep Dog that had escaped from a puppy mill in a nearby county, and she appeared to be very pregnant! The owners did not want her back, so someone called the Humane Society to see if they could take her. Of course, they said yes, but they simply had no space available in the shelter for her and the soon to be born puppies. Sharon knew I had a nice kennel with a dog house, long run with a cover and large fenced in play area, so she called Connie to ask if she thought I would allow them to put the dog there until they could make other arrangements. Connie told her she only had to call and ask if I would allow them to use the kennel.

Sharon called and we talked about the situation. Sharon asked if it would be possible to bring Shelly here to stay in my kennel, and I told her I did not think I would be able to take care of her and the babies when they were born since I was going into the hospital that afternoon for surgery on my back and would not be able to care of them. Sharon said that would not be a problem since the dog family would be cared for by the volunteers who would come out twice a day to feed and take care of their needs, clean the kennels. I would not have to do anything. I agreed, and later that day, Shelly was brought here and placed in the kennel. She was beautiful, and I fell in love with her immediately! I went into the hospital that afternoon, had the surgery and came home two days later. While I was away, Shelly gave birth to eight puppies!

The next afternoon late, when the volunteers came to feed the family, they put all eight of the puppies in a box, brought them into the house and dumped eight squirming puppies on the foot of the bed where I was lying! They were two days old, constantly squirming around and making mewling sounds. I was hooked! They were simply precious! One of them kept shuffling until he made it all the way to my neck, got as close as he could and latched onto to me. He chose me and I named him Spencer!

Now this could be a problem! I had fallen heir to a large, not in good shape German Shepherd named Zeus, and he and I were very close. He considered himself my protector and when I went outside with him, he followed every step I took! I was concerned that he might jump into the kennel and hurt Shellie and the babies! That didn't happen! Zeus took on the job of being Daddy to the family! If any forest animal came close to the kennel, he had a fit, chased

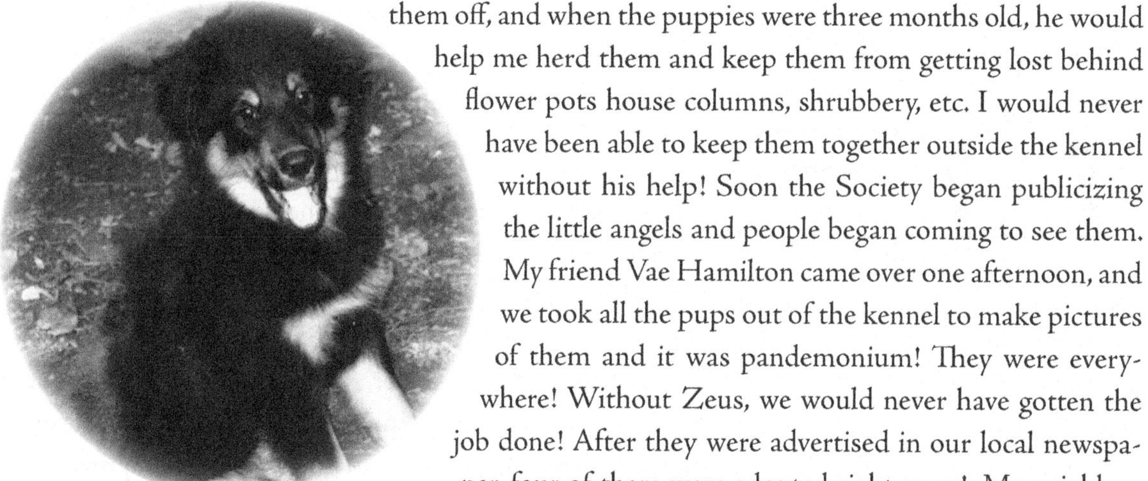

His Royal Highness
Spence the Magnificent

them off, and when the puppies were three months old, he would help me herd them and keep them from getting lost behind flower pots house columns, shrubbery, etc. I would never have been able to keep them together outside the kennel without his help! Soon the Society began publicizing the little angels and people began coming to see them. My friend Vae Hamilton came over one afternoon, and we took all the pups out of the kennel to make pictures of them and it was pandemonium! They were everywhere! Without Zeus, we would never have gotten the job done! After they were advertised in our local newspaper, four of them were adopted right away! My neighbor, Neil Crandall, decided to adopt one of the puppies, and he named him Red, because he was a gorgeous red-blond color: just beautiful. In fact, all eight of them were gorgeous. Three looked like Shelly, three were mostly black and white and two were red blond! Neil asked if Red could stay with me until he could get a fence built around his yard. Of course I said yes, so Spencer, Red and the remaining pups remained in the kennel and were often brought into the house.

After a couple of weeks, Neil decided to move back to Vermont where his children lived and he could not take Red with him, so I had Zeus, Red, and Spencer! When the volunteers came to pick up the remaining puppies, I made the decision to not keep Spencer. I had promised Neil I would take care of Red and didn't think I would be able to take care of three large dogs. I thought they would be too much for me to handle, so I let the volunteers take Spencer and the two remaining pups to the local pet store to be adopted! Minutes after they left, I fell apart! The thought of not having Spencer was simply too much! I had gotten so involved with him, I could not bear to not have him! I jumped into my car, drove like a maniac to the pet store, jumped out of the car, ran into the store and found a little girl holding him! I asked to see him, then ran to the volunteers and said I was adopting him! He, Red, Zeus, and I became a very close knit family for many years. It was the best decision I ever made! Nearly everywhere I went the boys went with me.

They became known by many people who thought of them as my kids! When I had to go out of town my wonderful friend, Linda Connor, would stay with them. Linda loved them as much as I did. The years passed and suddenly tragedy struck! Zeus became very sick and had to go into the hospital. A few hours later the hospital called and said Zeus was in critical condition with kidney failure and must go to the Veterinary School Hospital in our state capital in Raleigh, North Carolina. At 3:30 in the morning the boys and I drove to the clinic, picked up Zeus and began the three hour drive to Raleigh. The drive was difficult. I had to drive with my left hand and hold Zeus's IV high in my right hand! The boys were absolutely cooperative and quiet on the trip. Thank God there was very little traffic on the Interstate that time of the morning! On arrival, Zeus was rushed into intensive care in the hospital and treatment began. After a while I was told that Zeus was in very critical condition and that I must leave. The doctor recognized we were a close knit family and he thought Zeus would use his strength to put up a good front for me instead of using it to help himself! I told the doctors to do whatever was necessary to save Zeus!

The boys and I left for home and about two hours into the trip my cell phone rang and the doctor told me Zeus had passed away during surgery! I was devastated! The doctor asked what he should do with Zeus's remains, and I asked him if there was a good animal crematorium in Raleigh, and he said there was. Twenty four hours later, the crematorium called to say that Zeus was ready, and how did I want his cremains sent to me. I told him Zeus was born in dignity, lived in dignity, and would come home with dignity! I said I would pick him up later that afternoon. The boys and I got into the car and drove back to Raleigh to bring Zeus home. Later when my friend Vae Hamilton heard of Zeus's passing, she did a beautiful watercolor painting of him and it now hangs in my kitchen. Vae, like me, is a real lover of animals! Zeus now lies in a beautiful wooden box with his name and date of death on the cover.

So life went on. Spencer, Red Dog and I, along with lots of Zeus' friends grieved over losing him. Spencer and Red Dog became more and more important to me and we were together all the time. We've made many trips together, and the boys, became famous for their intelligence, calmness, devotion to me, and to each other. And their language ability! I trained them in French! From their birth, I spoke only French to them! I really don't know why I began talking to them in French, but I did, and they were famous!

His Royal Highness
Red the Great Houdini

Years passed and Red, Spencer, and I had a wonderful life together. We went on weekend trips to the beach and to the mountains, and to the dog park nearly every day where they had lots of doggy friends with whom they could have a good time. Of course we adults became good friends, too, cheered each other up when one of the dogs got sick or passed away. Time passed, and my sweet Red got very sick with colitis, and in spite of special treatment, he passed away. He was only 11 years old. All the dog park friends were here with us when the Doctor came to help Red cross the Rainbow Bridge. Spencer was never the same after his brother died. About two years later, I took Spencer to the veterinarian 's office to get bathed. When the attendant got him up on the table, he slumped and could not get up. I was called, went rushing over there, and brought him home. Then I called Dr. Suzanne Sewell who had taken care of the boys almost from birth, and she drove all the way from Marion, a town about an hour away, during a raging thunderstorm. There was nothing she could do for him. He'd had a stroke. So Spencer, with her help, crossed the Rainbow Bridge to be with his bother Red, and his dad, Zeus. He was 13 ½ years old. My heart was broken! Since then I have not been able to get another dog! You cannot replace perfection! So now I take care of my forest friends and live with the memories of three of the most wonderful creatures born who will always live in my heart! I miss them every minute of every day!

Not long after Spencer passed away, I began seeing some stray cats roaming around our fenced in swimming pool, and I began feeding them. There were seven of them and eventually five adult raccoons and two skunks joined them! What to do? A few days later one of the raccoons began bringing her babies for their evening meal. Their food supply became more complicated! The baby raccoons needed a different food. So I bought kitten food, put it into smaller bowls away from the adults bowls, and, yes, the adults began eating the kitten's food! What a dilemma!

At about that same time one of the female cats had a litter of kittens, and when they were old enough she began bringing them to the food bowls! What to do? They needed their own food. Finally I decided to put smaller bowls of kitten food on the pool house porch. The adults found that, too. Then I put the smaller bowls behind the sofa on the porch and that worked! The kittens liked to play there and the larger animals could not get behind the sofa!

The food situation wasn't the only problem! I had a gallon bucket that I kept filled with water for all the animals. When the raccoon mother began bringing her family in the evening, to eat and drink, the little ones were having trouble drinking from the bucket. One day, two of the babies jumped on the rim and began drinking. The third baby tried to get on the rim and in the process knocked his brother head first into the bucket! The mother just kept eating! The baby could not get out of the bucket! The two little ones fell off the rim and began jumping and screeching. I happened to be passing through the bedroom and saw what happened! I grabbed a towel, ran out, pulled the baby out of the bucket, shook the water off him the best I could and then wrapped him in the towel. The mother finally finished her meal and came to me, inspected the baby, picked him up, circled around my feet and walked away. I was one shaken lady! After that happening, the raccoons were not scared of me, would come close and let me pet them!

One day I went out to feed the animals and did not get the sliding door to my bedroom closed all the way. I put in place all the bowls, then picked up some trash from around the pool and went back in the house. I picked up some dirty clothes from the bench at the foot of the bed and I walked down to the hall to the kitchen. When I got to the kitchen door, I saw two small, baby raccoons standing at the base of a very wide wall of windows! I slipped quietly around the kitchen island, got some grapes from the refrigerator, squatted to the floor behind the babies, and said, "HI!" The little ones waddled over to me, took a grape, and very slowly I backed all the way to the bedroom door, doling out grapes to the babies! I stood up, opened the door, went out and the babies followed me! After that all the so-called wild animals were very relaxed with me unless there was a stranger or two with me! After that happening the other not so wild things let me pet them! There is always something interesting going on around here with all the wildlife! Lately, though, the cat population is diminishing.

Over the years I have been having the females spayed so there are not nearly as many as there used to be. One kitten was the only one remaining of a litter I did not know had been born and the mother has disappeared. Apparently the foxes, coyotes, and other wildlife are slowly killing off the cat population. That is disturbing! But there is nothing I can do!

Over the years, there have been many happenings with the wildlife. The deer population changes every year. New babies are born, every Spring, the various adults migrate, and some get killed by traffic on our busy road. Fortunately, my house is built on about 15 acres of forest and adjoins nearly 500 acres owned by friends and no hunting is allowed. The landowners donated several acres to their family member who, along with her husband, built and opened a Montessori School! It is wonderful to see all the children running and playing on their beautiful playground!

Zeus

Spencer.

Red.

The cats are just as interesting to watch as are the deer. I feed them twice a day. The first thing I do when I wake up is open the draperies that cover the entire wall of windows overlooking the swimming pool and patio. Sitting side by side in a line are raccoons, skunks, cats and kittens and an occasional opossum! They sit quietly while I open the sliding door and set down about a dozen small plastic bowls filled with cat food and table scraps in a long line close to the house.

Recently, the cat numbers have changed, and I think we have an active coyote in the woods who is killing some of the animals. For instance, I had a beautiful yellow/orange striped male cat that was recovering from a broken leg and being neutered. He went missing along with a pregnant black and white female due to deliver any day. She was scheduled to be neutered as soon as the babies were about three months old. She must have had the babies because suddenly a tiny gray kitten but no mother or brothers or sisters showed up at the house. The remaining cats are taking care of him/her, and I put out special food for the baby. But, I think we have a coyote that is killing lots of wild life, and they must be getting the cats also. The cats all live in my barn. They all have beds and can bury themselves in the blankets in fresh hay during the winter. It is like a three ring circus around here and I love it! Unfortunately, with the cat population diminishing, there may not be any left!

My bird population varies from season to season. Right now it is very cold and a lot of the birds have migrated. Between the birds and the squirrels still here, my critter food bill is nearly as much as mine, but it is worth it to see all the activity outside my bedroom sliding door! I just pray that whatever critters are taking my pets soon find another food source!

THE MAN WHO THINKS HE CAN

If you think you are beaten, you are
If you think you dare not, you don't,
If you like to win, but you think you can't
It is almost certain you won't.
If you think you'll lose, you're lost
For out of the world we find,
Success begins with a fellow's will
It's all in the state of mind.

If you think you are outclassed, you are
You've got to think high to rise,
You've got to be sure of yourself before
You can ever win a prize.
Life's battles don't always go
To the stronger or faster man,
But soon or late the man who wins
Is the man who thinks he can.

—Walter D. Wintle

ATTITUDE

The longer I live, the more I realize the impact of the attitude on life. Attitude, to me, is more important than facts. It is more important than the past, than education, than money, than circumstances, than failures, than success, than what other people think or say or do. It is more important than appearance, giftedness or skills. It will make or break a company...a church...a home. The remarkable things is we have a choice every day regarding the attitude we embrace for the day. We cannot change our past...we cannot change the fact that people will act in a certain way. We cannot change the inevitable. The only way we can do is play on the one string we have, and that is our attitude...I am convinced that life is 10% what happens to me and 90% how I react to it. And so it is with you...we are in charge of our attitudes.

—Charles Swindoll

LEARNING FRENCH

Have you ever heard the expression "Don't wave a red flag in front of a bull unless you are ready for action?"

One late afternoon in 1981, while shopping for groceries, I spotted a local newspaper, the *Hickory Daily Record*, on the newsstand. "Uh oh" I said to myself. The headline said, Lenoir-Rhyne College had a new intensive language program. I bought the paper and finished my shopping, ran a few more errands then drove home. As soon as the groceries were put away, I made a cup of tea and sat down to read the article.

Lenoir-Rhyne College was one of six colleges and universities awarded the Exxon Education Foundation's IMPACT (Implementation of Materials and Procedures Affecting College Teaching Program).

Approximately eighty-seven students had attended the three-day workshop at Dartmouth College, now a university, in Hanover, New Hampshire, sponsored by the Exxon Foundation. During the workshop, the representatives from each college and university competed against each other to receive the $6000 grant to implement the Dartmouth Intensive Language Model at their institutions. This model was a highly successful teaching model developed by Dr. John A. Rassias, Professor of Romance Languages at Dartmouth.

Following the workshop, Dr. Bohdan Kuropas, who was representing Lenoir-Rhyne College, received notification that Lenoir-Rhyne was awarded one of the six impact grants. The grant was used to implement the "Dartmouth Intensive Language Model" into Lenoir-Rhyne's program of instruction in its foreign languages – French taught by Dr. Bohdan Kuropas and Dr. Augustin Quilici, Spanish by Dr. Robert Eckerd, and German by Dr. Werner Schulz. Dr. William Keller was the head of the language department.

This method of teaching was almost a total immersion. The French students were in the master class with either Dr. Kuropas or Dr. Quilici for one hour every day, one hour in a laboratory session, and one hour in a conversation session every day. This allowed the student to achieve six hours credit at the end of the first semester, and satisfied the college's language credits required to graduate. And the college hoped if one would work hard enough, he or she would be able to speak, read, and write their chosen language good enough to carry on decent conversation.

Now, why would a 42-year-old woman with a family want to learn another language? Stupid, right? Nope. For several years my family had hosted teachers from different countries for a visit through an exchange program. These teachers stayed most of the summer in order to learn better English and more about American customs and for us to learn more about theirs. I chose France, so our first guests were Jacques and Jacqueline Bans from a village near Paris: Mantes-la-Jolie. Jacqueline spoke excellent English, was an English teacher but her husband Jacques spoke very little English. Jacques was a funny, funny, as in hilarious man. His trying to learn English kept my children laughing and me trying to speak what French I had learned so far added to the fun.

One evening we took them to a restaurant, Mom and Pop's Fish Camp, located in the small town of Claremont nearby. It was necessary for Jacqueline to translate the menu for Jacques. He decided he wanted a fish platter. I explained that it was a very large plate with lots of food on it and Jacqueline translated for Jacque. He rubbed his stomach and said, "I am hungry." When the food came and he saw the platter overflowing with food he said, while rubbing his stomach, and mixing English and French, said, "My eyes sont plus grand que mon estomac." Translation: My eyes are bigger than my stomach. We all had a good laugh with him, and he managed to eat half the food. When we had all finished our meal the waitress asked Jacques if he wanted a doggy bag. He looked at Jacqueline and asked what she had said. Jacqueline was not familiar with that phrase, so I explained it to her then she translated for Jacque. With a shocked look on his face he said, "Mon Dieu. En France j'ai un chien, mais les aliments se gateraient avant mon retour en France.

Translation: "OMG. In France I have a dog but the food would be spoiled before I return to France."

The remainder of their visit was fun since Jacques had such a good sense of humor. We visited several places not too far away and spent some time in our beach home in Seabrook Island, South Carolina, near Charleston. We visited homes of friends, went to museums, just doing everyday things that they enjoyed. Several times after their going home I visited them in their home in Mantes-la - Jolie. They are like family.

The next summer we had another teacher from France, Madame Nicole Morange. Nicole taught English in a private girls' school in her town and spoke English with a British accent. My kids were fascinated with her and how she spoke English. We made several short trips to various places, had lunch with my friends, and I learned a lot more of the language with her helping me. Over the years after her visit with my family I visited her family many times. Her son, Stephane, is now 40 years old and has two beautiful children, Appoline and Jean-Maxime.

Once when I was visiting the family, Pierre, who is a scratch golfer, wanted to teach me how to play. Pierre's pride was his beautifully landscaped yard with the grass resembling a perfect green velvet carpet. He put a golf ball on the tee, placed a ball on it and showed me how to swing to get the ball off. WHAM! I hit the tee, not the ball, the ball flipped into the grass, the tee broke into two pieces and a large chunk of his beautiful lawn came up.. Very calmly, Pierre put down another tee, placed the ball on it and wham. The same thing happened. After many tries and broken tees, and holes made in his beautiful yard, he finally said, "C'est assez. Je suis desole, mais, Je ne veux pas un tunnel a Chine dans ma Jardin." Translation: "That's it. I don't want a tunnel to China in my yard." I had no idea that I would have finished the program almost fluent in French, became good friends with both professors, and could go to France without any language difficulty at all except, of course, my pronunciation. Those three years were wonderful and opened the world to me. I became a globetrotter.

However, before that, my family had sponsored several European students during the summer. The first to come were two young ladies from France, Clarisse and Maria. The house was hopping with these girls, my kids, and their friends. This continued for a few years and the last high school group we had was the four teens. What happened during the three years of study? The fun began when I went to the college to register. It took four trips around the square before I got up enough nerve to go inside the gymnasium. My arrival in the parking lot driving a bright red Mercedes 560 SL sports car, created a sensation among several young male students who had also come to register. They were hooting and yelling and gave me a thumbs up. We talked a few minutes then went inside the gym. There were several tables set up and attended by students and teachers.

I spoke to the young woman at the info table and said, "My name is Pat Viles, and I would like to register for the beginning French class. She pointed to a table toward the back of the room and said, "That is Professor Bohdan Kuropas, and he is one of the French professors. He will teach you French." With great trepidation I approached his table, identified myself, and said, "The young lady at the info desk told me you could teach me how to read, write, and speak French in one semester." His reply was perfect. He said, "I sure can." If he had said, "I will try," I would have turned and walked away. This was the beginning of a friendship that has lasted more than 35 years. And so, another chapter in my life began, and I had no idea how much it would change me and my life.

When I left the gym that morning, the same group of young men were standing around my car admiring it. We talked for a while, and one of them said, "Gee, I would love to drive a car like this just once." I handed him the keys and said, "Let's go." I got into the passenger seat, and he drove around the block a couple of times. For the next hour, those young men and I drove around the block, and then they took me to lunch. Because of that action, I became notorious on campus for being a good sport.

On the appointed day, I entered the Rhyne building where the language classes were being taught, found the correct room with 12 students just out of high school already seated. The only available seat was front row center, and it took a lot of nerve for me to sit there and not run out of the room. I was literally scared speechless. I looked around and decided if those kids could do this so, could I. We introduced ourselves and were chatting when the professor came in, the same one with whom I had registered. He said "Bonjour. Je m'appel Dr. Bohdan Kuropas et je sera vos professor cet semetre."

And so, the classes began, and every day was a new experience for me. I have always loved to learn and something new was like a tonic. Being with much younger people and sharing experiences with them was fun, but a bit daunting. The professor was the best I had ever encountered, and he made learning the language fun. However, it was difficult, and I was struggling. At the end of the first two weeks, I felt that I would never learn enough to travel to France alone. I went to Dr. Kuropas and said, "I have tried very hard but don't think I am making progress, so I won't be back." I had never dropped a class before and did not feel good about it. Dr. K answered by saying, "You are really doing better than you think so give me just one more week." I agreed to come back, and we continued like this for several more weeks with my saying I wouldn't be back and him saying give him one more week.

Since this was a two semester course in the same time span as a normal semester, we could not take another course. After eight weeks, we had a week off between these two semesters. This course was designed to be intense. Before I left the classroom that day, I told Dr. K I would not be back. His response was, "Well, you have given it your best shot, but I think you are making a mistake. Learning another language is not easy, and at some point, if you stay with it, suddenly it will be like a light turning on, and you will understand. Do keep in touch."

My husband, Art, had a business meeting in New York City on Monday so we flew there. While he was in meetings, I would walk along 5th Avenue looking in the windows, have lunch and just enjoy the atmosphere. One day, while waiting for a traffic light to change, I heard two ladies in front of me talking, one more than the other. Suddenly, they were laughing, and I was too. One of them had been telling a joke, in French, and I understood. We introduced ourselves and ended up in a coffee shop, and I was able to talk with them in French. Hallelujah. The next Monday I was back in class, and Dr. K said, "Welcome back." If he had said, "I told you so," I would probably have left, but once again, he said the correct thing. Three years later, I left the college and never looked back and have remained friends with him and his wife, Lydia, and I became a citizen of the world.

Those three years were a riot. Since there were two French professors, we all had classes with both at different times. Dr. Augustine Quilici, the other French professor taught us how to interpret the symbolism in French Literature. There was also another adult in the program: a medical Doctor whose impetus for learning French was to go to France to learn about wine, and the two of us gave those young kids a run for their money.

In our second year, we were in a class with Dr. Quilici studying *Explicacion De Text Literaire Francaise*. Since much of French literature is written in symbolism, this class was to teach us how to understand what we were reading. One morning, Dr. Q told us we were going to have two young women visit to learn about the Darthmouth method of teaching a foreign language. They were from The University of North Carolina, would be graduating in two months, and would then begin teaching French. He told us to just talk with them, ask them questions, and answer theirs.

When the young ladies arrived, he introduced them, explained how the Dartmouth Model worked then left the room. He did not go for coffee. He left the door slightly ajar so he could hear what was said. There were only seven of us in the class, and we were a rowdy bunch. Questions from us were flying around the room, and the young ladies got upset and left crying. We had blown them away. Dr. Q talked with them a few minutes before they left. Then he came back in our classroom. He said, "Congratulations. You made me very proud of you today. Thank you." I have often wondered if those young ladies ever got around to teaching. Hey! We just did what we were told to do.

So, time passed, we learned, became good friends, especially Sarah and Christy. Sarah went on to law school, passed the bar and became successful working in Washington, D. C. Christy married a young man from Alaska, where their families lived, later divorced. She then married again, had two children and her family grows grapes and makes wine somewhere in Virginia. And another student, a little older than the high school age kids, Ali Mesfoui, from Morocco, was in all the classes too. His father, at that time, was Morocco's Ambassador to Turkey. He and I became friends and he spent time with our family.

About that wedding…My husband, daughter, and I decided to fly to Anchorage, Alaska, to attend the wedding of Christy and her fiancé Ben, who is the son of then Senator Ted Stevens. We flew from our home in Hickory, North Carolina in a small plane to the Charlotte airport to pick up our Alaskan flight and my suitcase did not get transferred from the small plane to our Alaskan flight in Charlotte. Unfortunately, all the clothes my daughter and I would need for the week were in that same suitcase. The trip was on the day before Thanksgiving that year. There was a family dinner that evening including out of town guests, and my daughter, Janelle, and I had no clean clothes to wear for the occasion and it being Thanksgiving, every store was closed. We went anyway and had a wonderful visit with the two families.

The next morning Mrs. Stevens called the Nordstrom Store and told them our situation. Two ladies came in, totally outfitted my daughter and me for the remainder of the week, altered things to fit and everything was on sale. Whoopee!

The wedding was beautiful, the guests amiable, the food wonderful and afterwards we made a tour of the surrounding area attractions. One outstanding visit was to a Russian cemetery. The graves had tiny little houses at the head instead of crosses or plaques. Very interesting. After that we visited the art and history museums, the library and met some wonderful people. The landscape was gorgeous with all the snow. During this trip the Northern Lights never could be seen. The sky was dark gray with rain and snow falling. Unfortunately, my husband had to return home for a meeting, so we did not get to see them.

Later in October of that year, I traveled with my mom to visit her grandson and my nephew, Jeff, in Fairbanks, Alaska. Jeff was in the Air Force and had been stationed there about six months. The first evening we were there I kept going outside to see if there were any of the Northern Lights. It had been raining and very cloudy all day and I prayed I would be able to see the Northern Lights just one time. After dinner, around 7 pm, I went out again and was met by the most gorgeous sight on the horizon that one can imagine, and one I don't think I will ever see again. That is a phenomenon only seen about 20 times a year, and it was the beautiful deep red-orange lights lighting up the horizon as if it was on fire. And there they were. They seemed to be pulsating in a very strange rhythm. It was a life changing experience. I ran back into the house, grabbed my mom's fur coat, got a thermos of hot chocolate, a folding chair, and ran back outside where I stayed most of the night watching the gorgeous light patterns that appeared. There were different shades of green threads in a cascade of the shimmering veils, a mushroom looking formation in shades of silver and green and they were red at the horizon. All during the night, the lights kept changing. It was magnificent.

A few days later, we were scheduled to fly back to Fairbanks to take our flight home. When the plane ascended, the pilot came on the speaker and told us that beautiful Mount McKinley was visible, and we could see it. Here again is a phenomenon seldom seen because of the almost always low hanging clouds. The pilot had permission to fly around so we could see all the glaciers with sunlight bouncing off them making shafts of beautiful glittering light. Before my nephew was moved back to an Air Force base closer to home, Mom and I went back two more times, but I never saw the red lights again.

After this trip, Dr. K and I decided we would go together to learn Spanish. We registered and were looking forward to the classes that would be taught the same way as French. The first day was a shambles for me. Dr. Eckerd commenced by going around the class, introducing himself, learning our names and why we wanted to learn Spanish. He began the same way Dr. K. had done in the French classes. When he came to me, he snapped his fingers, pointed at me and in Spanish asked me my name. The next words out of my mouth were French. I had become like Pavlov's dogs! Word got around the campus so other students would sneak up behind me while I was in a crowd and snap their fingers just to hear me speak French. It took a while to get out of that mode, but the entire campus had a wonderful time teasing me. Of course, after a while, I didn't respond in that way anymore except on occasion to give the kids a laugh. It was not the right time to take Spanish, so I dropped the class, the first I had ever dropped, and I never got around to studying that language again but picked up a lot on trips to Spain when I went to paint. Really, with knowing how to read, write, and speak French, it was easier to understand and speak Spanish since the two are very similar. Of course, I made mistakes. Still do.

The three years I spent learning French opened the world for me and gave me families all over Europe. I learned that a smile could open doors, laughter can heal the soul, sharing your thoughts and in my case, artistic ability, made a world of difference in being accepted anywhere I went despite the language difference. I am so happy I had the chance to broaden my education in a school that puts their students first. There are not enough words to express how my life has been enriched in so many ways by so many people. I wish every woman and man in the world could have the same experiences I have had, and I hope that I have made a difference in the lives of the people I have met during my travels. Dr. Kuropas and Dr. Quilici were wonderful teachers who made learning fun and taught us more than a language. I thank God every day that I had the means to go back to school, the courage to do it, the health, and a family who understood my need to broaden my horizons.

Life is wonderful…with regret to tell you that Dr. Augustine Quilici passed away seven years ago. Dr. Bohday Kanopas left us in late October this year 2022. Both men were wonderful teachers. It meant a lot to me and changed my life. Thank you, my wonderful friends

Life is wonderful…

Visitors from Esparza, Costa Rica.

Exchange Students: Stephanie and Gregorie from France and Maria and Maxim from Spain.

EXTENDED FAMILY

After I finished my studies in French my husband, Art, our children Eric and Janelle, and I talked things over and decided to begin hosting students from other countries during the summer while school was not in session. We applied to the same agency who had assigned us the two teachers from France who had visited us in the past. The first two girl students to come were Clarissa and Maria who were also from France. We had a welcoming party for them, inviting friends of our children, and everyone had a wonderful time. Our swimming pool was almost always full with the two girls, our kids and their friends from school. We attended several summer outdoor activities, made trips to our small summer house on Seabrook Island, South Carolina, and spent time in the mountains not very far from our home. We had so much fun with Clarissa and Maria we decided to do the same thing the next summer.

The following summer we invited two teenage boys, Stephane and Philipe from France. Stephane was actually the son of one of the teachers we had the summer before, Madame Nicole Morange. All the same activities of the summer before were enjoyed again. Our kids had a wonderful time with them and so did their school friends. Our house was always full of kids including those of families we knew and some that were new acquaintances. The six weeks passed quickly and we were sad to see them go home.

The next summer we had four exchange students come at the same time since our kids would be away most of the summer. We chose Stephanie and Gregorie from France, and Sofia and Maxim from Spain. Oh boy, this house was rocking. I contacted my local friends who had teenagers the same age and once again the swimming pool was full of kids every day. I was kept busy preparing goodies for them as well as fixing enough food for the enormous appetites of the boys. After a few days we decided to take them to Disney World. Have you ever tried to keep up with four teens whose English was minimal, keep enough cash on hand to feed them, pay for rides, and buy soft drinks since it was so hot? Believe me, it was not easy but Art, my husband ,and I enjoyed every minute of the trip. Once we returned from that trip, we did not have to entertain them all the time. Parents of their new friends had them to their homes, they played tennis at the country club and were just ordinary teenagers. There were a lot of happy kids that summer.

The next year we decided to do something different. Our church was one of several that were sponsoring a working trip to Esparza, Costa Rica to build a small house for the pastor of the Methodist church there and his family. There were several from our church who went, both men and women. It was quite an experience. We loved every minute we spent with the church members, people in the community, and the children who helped us. With the help of the local home builders, we volunteers learned a lot about house construction. Let me tell you, I laid a lot of concrete blocks and had the rough, scarred hands to prove it. By the time we left Esparza, the house was finished, and the very excited family moved into their new home.

We kept in touch with our friends there and shortly after our return home, my husband and I decided to invite the pastor, family, and some of the young people to share the Christmas holiday with us. In Costa Rica, they would be having their summer season at that time, so the schools would be closed. The group would include the pastor, his wife and child, several teenagers, and one young couple. Plans were made, and they all arrived at the Charlotte, North Carolina, airport one Saturday afternoon just before Christmas. Some of our friends and church members pitched in and helped with the expenses. We were grateful for that. I cannot remember the names of the visitors, and I could not find the journal I had kept during that trip.

On the drive home from the airport, we stopped at McDonald's for lunch. What an experience that was. They had never been to a fast-food restaurant, never even heard of one, and it took a long time to explain the menu to them, what a hamburger was, and we entertained everyone in the place. My Spanish was minimal, so it was a very interesting situation. When our kids got home for Christmas, they enjoyed the teenagers, took them around to meet their friends, and on Christmas Day, my two sisters and their families who live close by, joined us. It was pandemonium with everyone talking at once, the guests trying to figure out who was who, two languages echoing off the walls and mounds of food being consumed. Afterwards, we thought it was the most fun Christmas we ever had. My two sisters were wonderful. They cleaned up the kitchen and dining room, and my husband and brother-in-law took care of sorting out boxes and Christmas wrapping paper after the gifting session. Because of the large group, the gifts were small, actually just a token, but loved by everyone. We sang Christmas carols and snacked on fudge and cookies all afternoon. It was a wonderful celebration.

Over the years, we have had many guests from other countries who have given us a different idea of cultures around the world. I am so thankful our family has had the chance to learn about their homes and way of life, and help them to better understand Americans. In another chapter, you will read about other foreign guests we have hosted over the years.

A Quote

"Travel is fatal to prejudice, bigotry, and narrow-mindedness, and many of our people need it sorely on these accounts. Broad, wholesome, charitable views of men and things cannot be acquired by vegetating in one little corner of the earth all one's lifetime."

—Mark Twain

CIRCLE OF FRIENDS

I stand in the driveway waiting to attend to their needs of Red Dog and Spencer. The wind is blowing through the trees with the sound of a thousand voices. It is cold and I am tired from the long journey from France, yet I am wrapped in a cocoon of peace, love, and tranquility.

A quick, out of character decision, a chance encounter, a need for answers, grief, roundabout connections, and the coming together of four people who became known as the four Musketeers. This is the stuff novels are made of and that is what happened on a cruise to the Eastern Caribbean where four people came together in mutual need of each other, to become a "CIRCLE OF FRIENDS." God bless Sylvia Browne.

It all began innocently enough when I saw Sylvia on the "Montel Williams Show" on TV one afternoon and learned about her planned cruise on the Holland American Lines. Just turning on the TV in the afternoon was a miracle for me and to immediately go to the website on my computer and sign up for a cruise, which I had never enjoyed before, was another miracle. But there are no accidents which was proven as my time on the ship progressed.

Just getting ready to go was a major operation, Red Dog and Spencer had to be boarded, packing had to be done, and I had to get myself to the airport. A friend told me about an excellent animal boarding facility near the Charlotte, North Carolina airport. I called them and made arrangements for the boys, packed my luggage, and drove to the airport. The boys were not happy to be left in a strange place.

Once on the plane, I relaxed and took advantage of the time to do some reading. The flight was smooth and getting on the ship was not bad either and my stateroom very nice with a king size bed, but, after being there for a few minutes I realized that in the middle of the large ship, I was alone, knowing no one, and I said to myself, "What the hell are you doing here?"

With great trepidation I went to the Lido deck for lunch. Walking around, I spotted what seemed to be a friendly face, introduced myself and asked if I could join her. Not a good idea as it turned out. She was very negative, so after a few minutes, I excused myself and went back to my stateroom to unpack my suitcase and prepare for the first session with Sylvia. At 7:45 pm, hunger drove me to the Vista dining room where I had an assigned table. The adventure begins.

There was one man at the table, and I sat next to him. We immediately began talking. When he told me his story, I knew without a doubt why I was there and so did he. Ray's wife, Jeanie, was injured in an automobile accident 11 years before and became a quadriplegic. Jeanie had passed away five months ago after suffering two bouts of cancer along with being paralyzed. We exchanged stories and were a bit put out when others began arriving to join us.

Giovanni was the next person to arrive. He told us he was a film maker and producer of the

"CSI" TV series. He was a handsome, gregarious man from Italy who spoke several languages and had led a very active life. I believed, despite what he said, he was planning to make a documentary on psychic phenomena. During one of the sessions with Sylvia, she told him he would make a documentary, but she did not say on what subject.

Irina, originally from Romania, had been in the USA for nine years. She was the next person to arrive at our table. She did not talk much but what little she told us was interesting. It was easy to see that she was not comfortable sharing with us. The dinner conversation was interesting and informative. We separated around 10 pm, Ray to his room, Irina to the evening entertainment, Giovanni to the casino, and me to my room.

The next morning, I searched out someone to have breakfast with and picked out Linda who was alone. I felt drawn to her. She turned out to be a fledgling artist who had a compulsion a few months before to paint portraits, found a teacher to help her, and has never looked back. After an hour it was obvious. We had known each other in another life, and we have stayed in touch since the cruise, talking on the phone, and she visited me once. All the attendees of the "Psychic Experience at Sea" were wearing badges so we could recognize each other. They were not necessary though since we were all drawn together.

The first session with Sylvia was that afternoon, and I saw a lovely blond lady and invited myself to sit with her and her friend Marion. I had seen the two of them earlier in the afternoon and was immediately drawn to them. The area was so crowded we did not meet, so when I saw them again with available seats around, I joined them. There was an immediate connection between the three of us and Ray, and we quickly became known as the Four Musketeers. The four of us sat together for dinner that evening and every meal after that. Gradually, during the week, Linda, her daughter Ceci, Ray, and Irina became a larger part of our lives. By the end of the cruise, we had formed a bond that will never be broken.

What I learned from this experience is as long as we breathe the breath of life, we will never be alone. We are surrounded by the ones who went before us. We can bring them to us when we need them. We can be sure that the answers we seek will be there for us if we only ask. I learned that the validation I need can be gotten from myself. I learned that the beauty of my paintings do not come from technique, but from my soul. I learned that no matter what goes on around me, I am complete. I learned that everyone I meet touches me in a positive way if I allow that to happen. I learned that it is okay to believe in whatever I choose and not let anyone change my beliefs if I don't want to.

There is a lot I could say about the sessions with Sylvia Browne, Colette Baron Reed, John Holland, and Sheila Hallmeyer, but one word says it all: Fantastic. One had to be there to appreciate these wonderful people and be open to what they had to say. They all work differently, and I saw many lives changed. I saw mothers have closure with the deaths of their children. I saw people get information that will enable them to continue their lives in a much better way. I saw men and women come to grips with the reality of their spouses' deaths and become secure in knowing they will always be together in spirit. I saw solutions given to people who had been seeking them for years. I got information on how to take better care of myself physically. I got validation for my work. I had the privilege of meeting people who made a positive difference in the way I look at things now. I became a much more open human being.

I watched Ray go from a man drowning in grief to a man full of life and secure in the knowledge he did everything he could for his wife and how special he really was. I watched Marion accept that her mother who is sick with Alzheimer's would transition soon and that she has done all she could to make that transition easier. I was there to see Marilyn wrap herself in the love of the group and renew her love for her husband and children. I was there when Linda realized that she was doing the right thing for herself. I learned the connection I shared with Ceci was our love of fun and our doggy companions. Ceci's dog, Kodi, died just before the cruise and now we know that he is hanging out with my wonderful Zeus, a beautiful German Shepherd I rescued, who passed away when he was only 9 years old. I was there when Irina realized she had a different path in life than she had planned. It has been amazing to keep in touch with some of these new friends. Though we are separated by miles, we will always be connected. We also know we will be together again in our next life.

This was written after the cruise, and these people, for the most part are still a part of my life. Marilyn and I exchange phone calls, write letters, emails and we have visited back and forth. About two years after the cruise, Ray married a woman who had been a family friend for many years, and I eventually lost touch with him. Ceci and her family moved to a faraway state and I hear about her and her family from her mom, Linda. Irina is another with whom I have lost touch. She was much younger than the rest of us.

The area where I live in North Carolina is blessed with many excellent artists. Seven of these are featured in their own chapter of this book, "THE MAGNIFICENT SEVEN," shortened to "THE MAG SEVEN." The group met frequently for many years to talk about art and just be together. Unfortunately, time and life in general has managed to interrupt our meetings and now we usually talk by telephone and see each other occasionally. I have been blessed in having so many delightful women who become an integral part of my life. I see them at social functions, openings at the museum and other events there. There are many more people I have met over the years who have enriched my life. Some I met in painting workshops, others through various activities like those at the Hickory Museum of Art. The museum is in the old Claremont High School building and is truly a spectacular museum for the size of our town. Over the years new buildings have been built and added to the block and it now houses the Science Center, Art Museum, Library, and Theatre. It is now called the SALT Block, and you know how important SALT is.

The director of the art museum, Jon Carfagno, who came as director about 5 years ago, immediately began turning the organization into a first-class museum. Jon is a very hard worker and has not rested until he put the museum on the map. His right hand is Clarissa Starnes, the associate director, and their supporting staff are wonderful and hardworking too.

Since this staff have been together the museum has undergone a spectacular change, and I think it one of the best in the South. The museum recently hung an exhibition of the work of Andy Warhol. We had people flying in on private planes, some coming in busloads, crowds of school children, visitors from many states, and residents of the city and state came in droves. There was much excitement. It was a fabulous exhibit and was followed by an exhibition of the gorgeous flower paintings by Paule de Longpre. These paintings were beautiful and his inspiration for doing them was his own garden. Each of the paintings had honey bees in it. My seven year old grandson, Aleksander, was fascinated with the bees and ran around counting them and came up with the number of 38 bees. I think he had more fun at the reception than anyone else.

My friend, Joann Wilfong, is almost a neighbor. She lives about a mile from me, and we manage to connect almost daily by phone, try to have lunch together at least once a week, and attend most of the museum functions together. We both have been alone for a while. Joann is an excellent pastel artist, and I am fascinated watching her hands flying over the painting as she works. Unfortunately, she is like me and has so many responsibilities with family, yard work, staying in touch with her grown children, grandchildren, and volunteering at the museum, she does not have much time to paint. One of these days soon I hope we can have a joint exhibition. For many years, she and her husband, Harry, had a business: a plant nursery, where they grew all sorts of plants and flowers in greenhouses and outside. After Harry became ill with a debilitating illness, Joann had a hard time keeping the business going, and eventually closed the nursery. Harry passed away a few years ago, and Joann has managed to keep her beautiful house and yard in excellent shape. I envy how it looks. Mine looks awful. I am surrounded by a forest and not much sun gets through the trees so the grass does not grow like it should and over the many years I have lived in this house, the yard has deteriorated until it is no longer a picture of perfection. What the heck. Neither am I. Oh well. You can't have everything.

Joann also likes to play bridge and meets with a group of ladies on Fridays for lunch and an afternoon of fun. Not me. I tried playing when my kids were young, and it just didn't click with me. I am more of an action kind of gal. I admire her for sticking with the elderly ladies every Friday afternoon. She loves being with them, and they have a lot of fun together.

I have been blessed to have had so many wonderful people in my life. Knowing them has enriched my life beyond belief. Some of these people go back many years and are scattered all over the United States, Europe, China, Japan, Korea, the Caribbean, Costa Rica, many of our states and Canada. And then there are the many artist friends I have here in North Carolina. How lucky is that.

QUOTES FOR ARTISTS, JULY 2002

The difference between one man and another is not mere ability...It is energy.

—Thomas Arnold

The trouble with your work is not usually what you think it is. Art represents the joyous terrors of our childhood.

—Steve Martin

Nothing of value ever comes from a rational decision.

—Kate's paraphrase from ART

There's nothing coming to consciousness except through pain.

—Carl Jung

A Wider Circle of Compassion. A human being is part of a whole called by us "Universe," a part limited in time and space. He experiences himself, his thoughts and feelings, as something separated from the rest – a kind of optical delusion of his consciousness. This delusion is a kind of prison for us, restricting us to our personal desires and to affection for a few persons nearest to us. The task must be to free ourselves from this prison by widening our circle of compassion to embrace all living creatures and the whole nature of its beauty.

—Albert Einstein in Ideas and Opinions 1954

Patience is overrated.

—Denise Hodges

We shall not cease from exploration and the end of all our exploring will be to arrive where we started and know the place for the first time.

—T.S. Eliot

To be successful, the first thing to do is to fall in love with your work.

—Sister Mary Lauretta

There is no such thing as great talent without great willpower.

—Honoré de Balzac

If it's a good idea go ahead and do it. It is much easier to apologize than it is to get permission.

—Grace Hopper

Keep your fears to yourself, but share your courage with others.

—Robert Louis Stevenson

Trouble brings experience. Experience brings wisdom. Wisdom brings success.

—Anonymous

It is only when doing my work that I feel truly alive.

—Federico Fellini

I don't want people to want to paint. I want them to have to paint.

—Anonymous

When you're through changing, your through.

—Bruce Barton

The History...

In May of 1893, a group of Waldenses, from the Cottian Alps of Northern Italy, settled on land located near the Catawba River in eastern Burke County in North Carolina, between the towns of Morganton and Hickory. The center of this community became the Town of Valdese.

The Waldenses were pre-Reformation Christians with a religious ancestry that dates back to the 12th century. For centuries these Waldenses were persecuted by armies from both the governments of Italy and France and the official church. This tiny religious sect was forced to take refuge in the Valleys of the Cottian Alps of Northern Italy and remained secluded in the rugged mountains until they received their religious freedom by the Edict of 1848.

With this new peace their number grew rapidly until their Alpine farms could no longer support them. They looked elsewhere and began establishing colonies in other parts of Europe, South America, and the United States. They migrated to New York City, Chicago, Missouri, Texas and Utah, as well as Valdese. The Valdese colony became the largest Waldensian colony in the world located outside of Italy.

In the beginning, the Valdese settlers tried to make their living off the land as they had in Italy, but the poor soil would not produce. They turned instead to manufacturing, and with the same spirit of survival and determination of their ancestors, began to prosper. Today, Valdese has a solid manufacturing economy because of their efforts.

The Town of Valdese incorporated in 1920 and elected its first mayor, John Long, who was also the groom in the first Waldensian wedding in Valdese.

The story of the Waldenses is vividly told in the outdoor drama, "From This Day Forward" presented by Old Colony Players each summer.

Learn more about the history of Valdese and the Waldenses by visiting our local tourist attractions: the Waldensian Heritage Museum, Waldensian Heritage Winery, P&W RR Museum, Village Park Mural, Rock School Art Galleries I &II and the Trail of Faith.

Waldensian Church in Valdese, North Carolina, originally from Italy. This painting was commissioned to honor the Waldenses being in North Carolina from 1893 to 2018.

ARTIST STATEMENT

Waldensian Anniversary painting commissioned by the Waldensian Church.

Most of my exhibits consist of mixed media paintings or in some cases, multi-media. The object is to emphasize creativity using several different mediums to achieve my objective which is to give my viewers something different to look at and think about.

Creativity is "the power to create, to cause to come into being." A created thing is unique, brought into being by imagination and using unusual techniques and ideas. In my work, I try to avoid the commonplace, routine or ordinary. My way of doing this is to use materials not usually used by other artists or by using materials in an unusual way, such as thin silk fabric hand painted, inked or dyed myself, different papers I paint myself, and anything I can use to embellish the surface of the support I choose, like gels, gesso, organic objects, or anything that will make a mark or design and at the same time be archival. I dearly love tactile surfaces.

Creativity is a vital and happy part of my life. I have found that in creating my expressionistic or abstract paintings I am forced to let my imagination have full rein. I must make "what if" an important part of my creative process yet not let the process itself take over. Sometimes all it takes to start the creative process going is a word, the sound of music, a sight I see, or something someone says, and I am off into a world of my own. Sometimes the most obscure thought can send me on an imaginative exploration, which results in losing myself in my work. It is when I am "lost" in my work that I begin to make marks that mean nothing but come from deep within my soul. The joy that comes from such an endeavor is the most sustaining influence in my life and is what I consider "making art" to be.

LISTENING TO THE SPIRIT

Stepping outside your box is scary, especially the first time! Anything that causes one to deviate from their normal is scary! Being led by other influences leaves one without control of what they are doing. That's scary! And that's what is happening to me in the studio.

This story began many years ago when I was first introduced to the pictographs and petroglyphs of the American Southwest. I fell passionately in love with them and became a searcher on the trail of every site I heard about. This search took me high up on cliffs and into deep canyons, each site sending a thrill through my soul! I love to stand in front of them and try to figure out what they mean and why I was so connected to them. Some sites were more spectacular than others. In order to reach the cliff wall, it was necessary to descend 1000 feet into the canyon and then hike three miles on a wide trail that becomes a raging torrent when it rains! It was very hot that day, but my friend, Vae Hamilton, and I were with a trail guide who provided us with snacks and water. While hiking the trail, our guide told us what we were going to see. Nothing she said prepared us for the vision that suddenly appeared before us! I stopped dead in my tracks, overwhelmed by the spectacular scene before me! The painted figures were awesome! Their size, some 15 feet tall, their age unbelievable: 5100 – 9000 BCE! I could not believe what I was seeing! I rubbed my eyes and looked again: nothing had changed!

The panel was 200 feet long and contained several figures. They are considered one of the finest displays of rock art in the Americas. They have been named *The Holy Ghost and his Family* and are considered The Sistine Chapel of the West. They were large, still colorful, but just a bit faded over the centuries, and overwhelming! I thought my heart would stop! How could they still be so magnificent after so many centuries? Our guide told us to stand as close to the cliff wall as we could and look up. We could not see the sky! The overhang was so great the glyphs were protected, so they did not fade over the centuries!

The colors in the cliffs with the sun shining on them, and the majesty of the place was overwhelming. Standing there, I felt very small yet very much a part of the spiritual aura surrounding the cliffs. I could have stayed there for hours just looking and taking in the Spirit of the place!

There are three other rock panels in the same area. Just before reaching the Great Gallery there was a site where there was a petroglyph of a line of children holding hands that reached several feet along the base of the cliff. Others equally as interesting were all around. It was difficult to take it all in! The Spirits were everywhere! I was covered with cold chills and could hear chanting echoing in my mind and throughout the canyon. I didn't think I would ever again be in another place that would cause the same reaction. I was wrong!

In 1996, an artist friend, James Louis Harrill, who had lived in Greece for 20 years, told me I should go there. Soon I would find myself in Crete! Another friend, Sheila Hollander, and I made our plans and went to Greece for two weeks. Beginning our stay in Santorini, we rented a holiday house situated on the edge of the cliffs and began wandering around the tiny island that used to be a volcano that erupted eons ago and made a crescent shaped island surrounded by turquoise water so clear you could see huge fish swimming and eating the smaller fish!

The beautiful small white homes, some with deep blue roofs and others bright red were gorgeous. The color in the cliffs that descend to the sea, the dazzling white of the houses, the blue, blue sky, the turquoise water of the Aegean Sea, and the unceasing sunlight made a beautiful panorama of color and patterns. During the day we heard the constant sound of hooves of the small horses and goats going up and down the steps that wove in and out among the houses. These animals were used to take supplies and loads of grain to where they were needed. The small houses and holiday cottages were built all touching each other. The window shutters and doors were painted like the roofs: the colors of the sky and red! Gorgeous! The vivid blue roof of the Monastery perched high on the hill, the houses stacked like boxes with their colorful trimmings and the scenery overlooking the sea was incredible! I could hardly wait to paint! I had been told that there were frequent earthquakes in that area and wondered how strong they were and how long they lasted, and if they came often. I didn't have to wait long to find out!

One afternoon I was sitting on the porch of our holiday house working on a watercolor painting when the house began shaking. My water container overturned spilling blue water on the white steps, my palette and brushes went over the wall never to be seen again! I jumped back so I wouldn't fall over the edge . The shaking lasted only a few minutes but scared the heck out of me! I don't remember where Sheila was at the time, and prayed she was okay and she was! She came running to see if I was okay We hugged and thanked God it was not a bigger display of nature's force. A little later, I realized the blue water I had been painting with that had spilled during the quake and had dried and left a stain on the white steps! I hurried to wash off as much of the blue as I could and hoped rain would wash off the remainder.

When we visited Akrotiri on the island of Santorini to see the archaeological ruins of the Minoan Civilization of 4000 years ago, I was not very impressed. They were sort of ho-hum, compared to what I had seen in the Barrier Canyon (Horseshoe Canyon) until we began to see the excavation shafts with the ancient pithoi, huge clay pottery storage containers with beautiful patterns decorating them, that had been excavated during the archaeological digs. This was my first introduction to the Minoan Civilization, which was to become a total fascination to me! While walking through the ruins, I began to have strange feelings as if I knew what would be around the next turn, as if I had walked these corridors before! I had the feeling of being on the brink of a great discovery, but nothing prepared me for what was to come!

We spent one evening having dinner in Ios on the side of the island where the sun sets with a spectacular display of light and color! The simple box like houses took on a pale orange appearance and the blue roofs darkened. After dinner it was time to rest and take the ferry back to the island of Crete to begin another part of our adventure.

The night ride to Crete was an adventure with torrential rain, thunder and lightening lasting a while. We watched other ships passing by with people looking out the windows at us as we did them, talking with the other passengers, learning where they were from, where they had been on their trip and sharing opinions about the places we had seen and the adventures we had. The sea was not too rough and on our arrival in Crete the rain had stopped. The city of Heraklion was a hillside of light, beautiful and entirely different from Santorini. Yes, the buildings were stacked on the hillside, connected in the main part of town but otherwise it was spread out like any city would be. We managed to find our holiday house without trouble and had a good night's sleep.

Our first visit was to the Candia Museum of Heraklion, and it was special. I was fascinated by the ancient artifacts I was seeing. Who were these Minoans? From where did they come? Why did I get a tingling feeling when observing certain things?

I needed to learn more, so I went to the gift shop and bought a book on the Minoan Civilization, found a corner with a bench and began reading. My fascination grew! When I saw the pictures of the Minoan frescoes painted over 4000 years ago my heart skipped a beat. My body was covered with chills, and it was hard to breathe! I could read no more, closed the book and continued going through the museum. Everything I saw seemed familiar. How could that be when I had never heard of the Minoans before this trip, never been in this museum before? This question was answered when I saw the frescoes! Suddenly I was shaking all over, had trouble breathing and was crying! I had to leave the room a while, go outside. When I returned to the fresco rooms, the same thing happened and once more I went out. After a few more tries, I could stay and really study the gorgeous murals I was seeing and realized I had found myself. Deep inside, I felt I had had a part in making these frescoes 4000 years ago and that was my first indication that I had lived before, probably many times, and most likely will live again in another life! That's scary! My fascination with these people continued, and I went back to Crete twice more and learned more each time.

According to the book I had bought, it is impossible to know for sure how the people reached Crete, a 152 mile long, whale shaped island in the Mediterranean. They were the most active, highly developed and cultured people of all the early civilizations. Is it possible to know for sure who they were, where they came from? I don't know! I don't think so. In my reading I learned they arrived sometime in the Seventh Millenium, BC. They were probably seagoing people from nearby areas, for instance the Levant, the Greek Mainland, today's Israel, Lebanon, and Syria. Huddling in their small boats, they would have been happy to see the beautiful mountain peaks before them! Those awesome peaks rose out of the ground like a powerful God!

These seafarers founded colonies throughout the Agean, developed the first Merchant Marine, built ships, learned how to make stone vases from the Egyptians, and how to make bronze from the Sumerians. They decorated their houses with scenes of flowers and birds, people relaxing, and people engaging in sports. Architects designed their harbor facilities, aqueducts, and palaces. Their achievements had no parallel to other parts of Europe!

Most people still lived as they had since to the dawn of humanity. They roamed in groups of clans hunting animals, birds, and gathering wild plants to eat. In other parts of Europe no one else had developed the kind of agriculture that would lead to surplus crops and the creation of a civilization! The Cretans accomplishments were almost unnoticed by history, and they were remembered only by myths until their accomplishments were discovered by Sir Arthur Evans who had seen tiny seals in antique markets. Thirty-three centuries later, when their secrets began to be discovered during the excavations of their palaces, their excavations uncovered jewelry, tapered columns, gorgeous frescoes depicting idyllic scenes, evidence of their religion which included worship of the Snake Goddess Gorgon, and bulls. He found many sacral horns of consecration and found evidence of writing systems: Linear A and Linear B of the Mycenaeans. Linear A has never been deciphered, but Linear B has.

Where do I fit into all this? Did I live as a Minoan? Was I a court artist who worked on the frescoes? Does this explain my passion for ancient scripts and the people who wrote them? Have I always been an artist? I don't know the answers to these questions. I only know that I had to do a series of paintings when I returned home from Greece and it seemed as if my hands were guided by an unknown source!

This seems to be a good time to say that one of the first commissions I received after this trip to Greece was from a family who collected my work and wanted a large painting for the foyer of the new home they had just built and moved into. It was a huge foyer and the wall behind the long sofa that would be there was nearly 12 feet wide! I told them I could not do a painting that large. I suggested they have a large folding screen built and painted by an artist I knew who could do it. The husband said, "No! We want you to do it!" I told him I didn't do screens and he said, "Well, you do now!" What could I say? After thinking about it a few days I agreed to try!

I introduced them to the Minoan frescoes, they liked them and a few days later a large truck pulled into the driveway and unloaded 6 beautifully wooden made panels, a total of 11 ½ feet wide and 9 1/2 feet tall! I nearly croaked when I saw them and wondered how in the world I was going to fit the panels on my work table. I cleaned it off, put a new plastic cover on it, and when the driver brought them in one at a time, he laid them side by side on the table that is 4 feet wide and 8 feet long! With not an inch of the table surface showing, and the screen, being 11 ½ feet wide and 9 ½ tall, it was jutting out on both ends and sides of the work table. There was barely room to walk around the table, and I, being only 5 feet 2 inches tall could not reach the center to paint! Thank goodness I had a small four foot tall folding ladder and it saved me! I had to get on top of the screen and do all the necessary drawing then stand on the screen, bending over to paint! I used scenes from six different frescoes, not copying them exactly. This project took 3½ months since I painted on both sides of the screen in case they decided to use it somewhere else. The family was very patient, did not come to the studio, call at all, or ask me how things were going when we met socially!

When it was picked up from my studio it was still in six pieces, and I was planning to go to their home and put gold leaf on the hinges when they were installed. When the lady of the house called to tell me it was ready, I told her I would be there the next morning. I don't know what made me do it, but before going to their home, I bought a small bottle of Liquid Gold just in case the leafing didn't work. When I arrived, the lad of the house met me at the door and said "Pat, you are not going to be happy! My husband moved the screen from the foyer and hung it on the wall in the family room! I almost fainted! When I saw it there, I cried! I had used many dfferent paints to achieve the effect of the lily king, the lion, and the two servants this is a real mess----noting correct here! bearing beautiful amphoras, walking. For that to happen the screen had to be a bit folded and he had done that. But the screen was just beautiful on the backside as the front and it would not be seen. I told him "I love you dearly, but I must say your taste is all in your mouth!" He laughed! After many years the screen is still hanging on the family room wall and looks great! Just enough folding of the screen was done to make it effective. Why did he move the screen? His answer, "If I pay that much for a painting I don't want to have to make a detour to see it every day!" I couldn't argue with that!

So, those experiences added to the ones I had in other places in foreign countries, and in our own Southwestern states have given me a different view of ancient history and a desire to know more. There are many other places in our world I would love to explore but they may have to wait for my next life! I am getting old! As much as I enjoyed the screen project, I doubt I will ever do another one.

MARILYN AND ANNE

There are no accidents! I have found that to be true over and over again. Some of the most interesting experiences I have had and people I have met were the results of a decision I made on short notice or just simply took a chance and it worked out. Meeting Marilyn Freeze was one of those times!

I had learned of a cruise to the Caribbean Islands on the cruise ship, "Zuiderdam," a Holland America Line. This cruise was featuring people involved in spirituality, past life regressions, readings from different leaders and simply getting better acquainted with ourselves! I had been on a cruise or two before, but that type of traveling was not my favorite. I did not like to be confined. However, I was hooked! I flew to Florida to meet the ship hoping to meet many interesting people. I was not disappointed!

After being summoned to the mustard station, I began getting acquainted with lots of others on the cruise and to learn their reasons for taking this cruise. We were all bunched together. I noticed a lovely lady with beautiful blond hair and was drawn to her. At the time I was meeting new people, talking to them, telling stories of my travels and listening to their interesting stories. I kept being drawn to the blond and her friend, Marion. I learned later she was experiencing the same vibes about me! On meeting new and interesting people, I do talk a lot, especially when they also have good stories to tell about their travels and want to hear about mine. It was fun for us to share our experiences and why we were taking this cruise. After a few minutes we were called into the meeting room, so I did not have a chance to meet the lady I had noticed.

Later that day when I went to one of the lectures, I saw her and her friend and asked if I could sit with them during the meeting, and she excitedly said "Yes!" I settled into the seat next to her, and that was the beginning of a friendship that has endured for many years, hundreds of telephone calls, visits back and forth, which is amazing since she lives in New Brunswick, Canada and I live in North Carolina, USA. We were inseparable for the length of the cruise, and it became a trip to remember. We spent every waking moment together, went to events together, sat together, ate together, and even had our picture taken together. Looking at the picture you would never believe we had just met! We were both grinning from ear to ear, realizing at the time we would become best friends.

Over the years we have talked with each other by telephone every week and sometimes more. We shared many stories, some of which were secrets and would remain secret between us. Marilyn has said she did not think she had ever laughed so much, and I agreed. Marilyn and I shared the same sense of humor. So, when I began writing this book, I asked her to please write her thoughts about the things we had done, places we had visited, interesting things we had seen and done, the visits we had with each other and shortly six pages arrived. What a memory she has! So many things she wrote about, I had forgotten, so it was a lot of fun to relive the trips and visits we had over the years.

After a few years of telephone conversations, we learned of a retreat to be held in Sedona, Arizona. We agreed to meet in Phoenix, rent a car and drive to Sedona where we would stay for the week, each of us having our own room at the hotel. It was a fun week of getting reacquainted and adding new memories and meeting others who think and feel the way we do.

After that trip we continued to stay in touch and soon Marilyn called to say she was planning a trip to visit me! What a wonderful surprise that was! My home is literally in the middle of a dense forest. We walked throughout the forest with my two dogs, and she fell in love with my very spiritual surroundings. Marilyn loved meeting my dogs and considered them the best part of her trip. Their names were His Royal Highness Red the Great Houdini, so named because he climbed fences and opened doors, and His Royal Highness Spencer the Magnificent, because he thought he was! These dogs were rescued when I fostered the mother, and her eight puppies were born in the kennel we had for our own dogs . At that time, though, I did not have a dog. On a whim I trained the boys in French which presented a problem for them later! Marilyn said, "Spencer never gave me the time of day and stayed close to you, but Red Dog laid on my feet every chance he got. I obviously felt a special bond with Red." During this visit Marilyn and I sat with a cup of tea and talked most of the time. We made a few short trips around my area, into the mountains, and the Biltmore House in Asheville, North Carolina.

According to Marilyn, the best trip we had together was to Arizona. We met at the airport in Phoenix and quickly picked up our rental car and drove to Page, Arizona. After a decent night's sleep and breakfast, we walked through the town. Marilyn had never seen so many churches in such a small area. She commented,"Is it a good sign that we are among so many loving Christians or a bad sign that, indeed, we are amongst a bunch of heathens that are trying to reform?" We had a good laugh over this. We loved Page. We stayed there for a few days and traveled all around that area visiting many interesting places. I asked Marilyn if she would drive a while and she agreed. The difference in miles and kilometers threw her off. The speed limit was 75 mph, but she was used to kilometers and there is a big difference in the two. We discussed the problem, and she did an excellent job driving.

Our first outing from Page was to Antelope Canyon. To get there we booked a tour and rode into the Canyon in the back of a huge the truck, fitted with benches. The guide talked all the way, telling us interesting stories about the past. To this day, the Canyon remains one of our most enjoyed and favorite of the places we have visited. It is a magical place with the sun beaming down spreading beautiful light on the different rock formations. And, like many Canyons in the

Southwest, the colors of the cliffs are spectacular: Orange, yellow., pink, purple, brown and very scenic. It is called "The Painted Desert." There are other interesting stories about the canyon that also has a slot canyon when, at certain times of the day, the sun beams down through the slot and makes a gorgeous sight on the ground level. It was beautiful!

The canyon was formed by water rushing through during the centuries, making striations, fantastic shapes and changing the cliffs into spirals, wedges, and animal shapes. Hoodoos, large stone formations, were everywhere. The atmosphere was weird! We felt like we were in a fairyland or even, in some areas, a nightmare! We stayed in the canyon a long time and took many photos. I will never again look at cliffs and rocks in the same way. When we went into the canyon, we were told that if it began raining, we had to leave immediately! In those canyons, water has only one way to go: UP!

Canyon de Chelly was wonderful! There were people walking in the canyon, Navajo Indians riding horses, and the Navajos' lived in rustic houses. In the middle of the canyon was a huge round rock. In times past the Indians would scale the rock and live up there so the soldiers who often came into the canyon could not get to them. They knew the soldiers would kill them! There was no food or water and they eventually starved to death. The Navajos believed the land in the canyon was theirs, but the solders took possession of it.

After visiting Canyon de Chelly we went to Newspaper Rock. This is a huge rock, part of the cliffs, where, over the centuries, the Native Americans painted and carved what we call petroglyphs and painted pictographs. These tell the stories of their hunts, paintings of the people, their other activities and their travels. They were fascinating to look at and try to understand what they were trying to convey. The Native Americans believe it is a wrong to copy them exactly since they consider them to be part of their tribal religion.

The next places we visited were the Vermillion Cliffs, Marble Canyon and Lake Powell. These were all interesting and scenic places. Color was everywhere! The cliffs were vermillion and the intensity of their colors ranged from pale red to bright, and rusty red in the shadows. Beautiful!!!

One of the most interesting things to happen on this trip was the fact that we were never alone! Every time we stopped, we had company. It was the most amazing experience. Our constant and unique companion was a raven. At first it did not seem to be such a big deal. However, as time went on, we realized that we were not alone. Was it the same raven following us or was it a different one each time? We will never know! It got to the point that as soon as we pulled into a parking lot, we would look for our companion and, sure enough, he/she would be there waiting for us. Weird!!!

Because I was so familiar with that area of the Southwest, we saw everything imaginable.

Several times we passed by a huge house that was built between two monolithic boulders.

It was amazing and we wondered how it would feel to live in that house. I don't think the family who lives there will ever have to worry about an earthquake! The Navajo women sat in front of their houses with their beautiful and different jewelry and crafts for sale. We had so much fun looking at and eventually buying some jewelry. The jewelry and leather crafts made by the local Navajo men and women were stunning. We had much fun shopping and buying their wares. The pieces I bought are still cherished by my family members after all these years. We stopped by the Colorado River and watched many fishermen try their hand at fishing. On another trip with my friend, Vae Hamilton, she and I went rafting down the river since heavy rain had filled the river bed. That was fun!

Marilyn was interested in the Navajo people, and I told her some facts about them. One was that they owned most of the land through which we were traveling and were strict about the speed limit. I was driving and made sure to use the cruise control. Marilyn took a photo of a sign that read 'LOTO, AMO, GUN, BEER" that was next to a sign that read LAW OFFICE. Marilyn's comment: "Okay, we are in the west!" The Navajo Nation tries hard to keep their tribal traditions. They and other Indian Nations believe the pictographs and petroglyphs are sacred so don't copy them. It is difficult to paint the glyphs since there are so many of them and all appear the same. Once I saw them, I could not get them out of my mind but consequently decided not to paint them.

We saw many beautiful cliff formations and canyons. Bryce Canyon was where we saw the beautifully colored hoodoos. Words can hardly describe them! Bright orange, deep ochre, dense shadows made the hoodoos look like a fairy land. When the sun hit the hoodoos, they were blinding, beautiful, and fascinating. Since I had spent so much time in that area, I knew the names of most of them. We drove through a tunnel where the road had been cut through the rocks. And the moment we stopped, there was our raven!

We continued to the North Rim of the Grand Canyon where we had a fantastic lunch in a restaurant that overlooked the Canyon. We spent the night there. It was amazing to get up early, have breakfast, then drive to the rim of Bryce Canyon. It was cold that morning, so we dressed accordingly. Marilyn was thinking I had lost my mind for taking her there until the sun suddenly rose over the rim, magic happened, and I could not have dragged her away! The sun behind the hoodoos gave them the appearance of being translucent. Light was bouncing all around. The hoodoos looked like they had been lit within. How could stone look so translucent? It was a highlight of the trip.

After that experience we traveled to Canyon de Chelly. We lucked out when our guide turned out to be the son of a Navajo chief. He was amazing. He told us many stories, and we were so interested in what he was saying, we hung on to every word. There was a lot to look at and, yes, our raven was there to greet us. After that we visited Newspaper Rock, an unbelievable, huge rock filled with pictographs and petroglyphs dating back hundreds and perhaps thousands of years. They were magnificent and told the story of the people of the past. The Navajo said it would be okay to make them up but after seeing so many thousands of them there was no way I could make up more! We also went to see the Petrified Forest and a couple more stops before continuing our voyage to Flagstaff. We stopped at an Italian pizza restaurant and by the line up outside, figured it would be a good place to have lunch. Marilyn told the waitress that her daughter collected menus from various places, so the lady left one for her to take, but said, "Don't flaunt it to the other patrons!" Marilyn said, "That might be a problem since the menu is nearly as big as me!" She is so funny!

After Flagstaff, we headed to Cottonwood to spend the night with my friends, Jim Scott and Ted Schmitt. We were in for a treat. Jim was an artist who taught painting workshops in many foreign countries and all over the USA for years until he passed away. I was with the two of them on many of those trips and we had a wonderful time. Really, Jim and Ted were like brothers to me. Marilyn liked both Ted and Jim but thought there was something special about Ted. Before retirement, Ted had been a schoolteacher, was on the school board and was the Superintendent of Schools in St. Louis, Mo.

A few years passed, and our need to see each other again was overwhelming. When Marilyn was here to visit, she had met many of my friends, one of whom was Tone Duncan who is originally from Japan. Tone and I decided to visit Marilyn, made plans, and flew to Saint John's, New Brunswick, Canada for a two-week visit. This was in August of 2010. During those two weeks we packed a lot of visiting and sightseeing local places of interest. We visited the small towns along the seashore, went to Sussex to see the gorgeous murals painted on the sides of the buildings, then had ice cream in the converted train station. We also went for an overnight visit to Georgetown to attend a performance of *Anne of Green Gables*. Tone told us the Japanese people had always been in love with Canada's dear Anne! I, on the other hand, fell completely in love with the beautiful green fields, unending rows of potatoes and the red, red soil that reminded me of home. Later, at home, using watercolors, I painted a few pictures of those fields. It is a beautiful place.

Marilyn's home is built overlooking the Bay of Fundy. Standing on the edge of the cliffs looking down you would never believe that, when the tides are in, the water comes within a few feet of the edge! They have 50 feet tides there! One day several of Marilyn's friends joined us on a day long boat excursion to see whales. As we left the shore, passing a lighthouse, we saw amagnificent Bald Eagle standing on top of a light pole to welcome us out to sea. We were not disappointed as we passed seals bathing on small rock islands, and when we arrived in the middle of the Bay, we saw several whales breach the surface to fill their bellies with smaller fish! The sky was filled with gulls and other sea birds hoping to take advantage of the fish the whales did not get. The Bay of Fundy is also known around the world for its delicious lobster, and we certainly had a feast. Tone taught Marilyn's husband, George, a few things about eating lobster. He had never seen anyone eat a lobster the way Tone did! Tone and I did not want to leave, but home was calling so we packed our suitcases and took our flight home. Tone and I talked about this trip for years!

A few years, many phone calls and emails later, Marilyn decided to visit me again. I was opening an exhibition of my paintings in the Hickory Museum of Art, Hickory, N.C. where I live. The exhibition was a retrospective covering 20 years of work and featuring paintings from the many places I had visited around the world. So, on September 8, 2016, she flew from St. John to Charlotte, North Carolina, to visit me and attend the opening reception. My cousin, Anne, from Houston, Texas was arriving at the airport before Marilyn's flight was scheduled to arrive. Her flight arrived on time, so we had time to catch up on family activities, etc. Marilyn's flight was late and when she finally arrived, she discovered her luggage was missing! This did not dampen her spirits since we were all finally together and had plans to fit as much in as we could during the next 10 days. We came on to my house and her luggage was delivered later.

Marilyn and Anne had come for a visit mainly to attend the opening reception of my painting exhibition at the museum and then to see and do some interesting things in my area. On the night of the museum reception, the three of us went early to be there when the first attendees arrived. As the crowd grew larger the noise level increased, and I was flitting around talking to everyone about my work and just enjoying the festivities. Marilyn and Anne were circulating, and I think they must have made the acquaintance of everyone in the room. An interesting observation by Marilyn and Anne was that my family really had no clue about my work or how extensive it was! They were blown away by the number of works being shown, and the size and intricacy of the paintings. The girls and my family enjoyed meeting other artists and the museum staff. It was a fun evening, but the real fun was yet to come.

After a few days of seeing local places we went to Hiddenite, a small village about 10 miles from my home. In this village is a gem and mineral mine where we could dig for buried treasure! The mine had buckets of dirt taken from the mine and we were shown how to use the sluice to look for semi-precious stones that might have been hiding in the dirt. It was so much fun, and we all found some stones that could be made into jewelry. Marilyn found a nice Citrine specimen that she had faceted and made into a ring. My find was a large Topaz that, when faceted, made a lovely necklace! Some people who see it think it is a monumental diamond. I wish! I don't think Anne found anything special and decided to not have any jewelry made of her findings. But we had a great time that day and returned home tired and filthy but happy! Marilyn had a large bag full of semi-precious stones and various rocks to take back home. She was concerned that she would have a problem going through customs, so she cleaned all the pieces carefully and got through customs with no trouble. Marilyn's young grandson also shares her love of rocks, and he was happy to receive some of the ones she found there. Later, for his birthday, I sent him a box full of individually wrapped specimens, and he had a wonderful time unwrapping them, treating them as if they were gold! It doesn't take much to make a kid happy! I understand how he felt. I have an extensive rock collection of specimens from all over the globe!

One day a few years later, I got an e mail announcing that John Holland and other mediums were once again planning a cruise with an emphasis on getting in touch with our departed loved ones and mediumship in general. There would be 29 practitioners, some famous and some just starting out. Marilyn and I decided to take the cruise, and it was the right thing to do. We both got a lot out of the sessions and learned more about ourselves and received messages from departed loved ones. There was a lot going on during the cruise with so many mediums practicing, so we had to make individual schedules but most of the time we would be together. We both chose Niki Jacobs for one of the sessions.

Niki was lecturing when she suddenly stopped, approached me and said: "What is your name?" I answered "Pat." She then asked if I had a thyroid problem, and I said I did. She asked for how long, and I told her a few months. She then said, "I have your Spirit Guide here, and he says you are not getting the proper treatment." I said I would check with the doctor when I arrived back home. Niki went back to lecturing, stopped again and returned to me. She asked, "Do you write?' and I said "Yes." She then asked if I was writing a book and I said I was. Then she said, "You must finish the book. It is an important book and will mean a lot to women all over the world." I was blown away! Something like this had never happened to me before, and I was shocked and a bit scared. How did Niki know so much about me? I had never seen her before that day! I had never heard about her before that day! I had never had anything like this happen to me before that day! Even Marilyn did not know I was writing a book! So, I am writing the book! This book!

In the latter part of the week Marilyn had a reading with John Holland and her father came through to her. The accuracy of that reading sent her on a quest to find out more about mediumship. She immediately signed up for a course that would begin as soon as she arrived back to her home. She is now a practicing medium! Oh boy! I hope she doesn't read me!

On the the last day we went on an outing with Denise Linn and Mayan Elder, Elizabeth Araujo, for a fire ceremony. This was a different and wonderful experience. We arrived at an ancient temple in the ancient Mayan village of Chichen Itza and walked through a canopy of trees to a meadow where the ceremony would take place. This was a very sacred place. With her knowledge, Grandmother Araujo, performed a ritual that had been performed many times to bring blessings to the Earth and to those of us attending. We all made a large circle, holding hands and Grandmother Elizabeth began talking and building up a fire in the fire pit using several different things representing the different seasons, colors that had special meanings, candles, etc. When she finally lit the fire, it was beautiful! The different colored flames were dancing in the clear blue air and when the fire began to burn down, she offered a prayer. It was one of the most moving experiences I have ever had.

Then, Grandmother Araujo asked if anyone one would like to speak. A lovely lady from Hawaii said she would like to offer a prayer from her people. She sang this prayer: it was beautiful.

For a few minutes after she finished the prayer, we all stood very quietly, still holding hands. It was then that my mother, who had died a few years before, came to me and said, "Now I understand!" That meant so much to me! Mother had a difficult time with me being so different! Marilyn and I were both moved by this experience.

The following year Marilyn had the opportunity to go to Florida to attend a conference of the class she had signed up for on that cruise. Of course, I had to go too! On the first day Marilyn was busy talking to all the other students she had met online. She was worried about me but soon realized that she had no reason to be! I was as busy as a bee talking with everyone and making new friends. Since then, our phone conversations have continued, and she has gotten more and more interested in her mediumship studies and is now able to do readings for others. Is she going to read me? I thank God every day that a chance encounter gave me a wonderful friend like Marilyn. I have been very blessed in my life to have made so many friends, visited so many wonderful places and have so many experiences most women never have a chance to enjoy. And finding Anne so late was a miracle and I am thankful she is in my life. Life is wonderful!

We hope that when my cousin Anne, who is coming for a visit in August to attend a special event our wonderful art museum is having, Marilyn can come too. Lord help Catawba County, North Carolina, if this happens! The three of us could do some damage out there! Anne has already made flight reservations to come for the event and I hope Marilyn can work things out to

Bryce Canyon hoodoos.

come too. She is not sure she will be able to come then. Unfortunately she couldn't join us. Anne and I, along with other family members, had a lot of fun that evening, but we missed Marilyn. Since then we have talked on the phone and are making plans to get together as soon as possible!

Now, about my cousin Anne! We did not know each other when we were children. I was born in Arkansas and so was she but we were in different parts of the state. Anne is from my father's side of the family. We used to take a train from where we lived in Oak Ridge, Tennessee to visit my mother's family in Arkansas and then go on to other places in Arkansas to visit my dad's family. I vaguely remember the train rides which took a long time! During those times airplanes had not been invented! Anne is several years younger than me. In fact, she had not been born yet when we made our first visits to Arkansas!

So it was a great surprise to get a telephone call from Anne one day, introducing herself and we finally had a chance to become acquainted. We made plans for her to come to my home for a week's visit and when we saw each other for the first time it was wonderful. It was like we had known each other all our lives! Since then she has made several trips to visit me and one of these days I must hop a plane and surprise her! Anne was here for five days in August of 22 to attend a special event honoring my friend Joann Wilfong and me for our many years of volunteering at our local museum: together it was 139 years! Yep! I am a very old person: 84 years old! Joann is older than me, but not much!

Even though Anne has visited me several times, we have not made any of the special trips to special places near my home that Marilyn and I have shared. But we have done interesting things together, and spent time visiting some places not so far away, like the mountains. Isn't it wonderful to finally become acquainted with family!

I really don't remember many details of those scattered trips to Arkansas when I was so young. My mother and father were the youngest in their large families and they were older when they met and married. They also left Arkansas soon after they married and seldom had the time or money to go back for a visit there. Both are gone now, and I am a grandmother and a great-grandmother! How time flies.

THE MAG 7

In the early '80s my family had just built and moved into a new house. The kids were teenagers and were always looking for interesting things to do. One day my husband announced he was going to buy a farm. He had always wanted lots of land and this seemed like a good chance to own some. After buying the land he suddenly decided to build a horse barn and buy some horses. His motivation was not clear, and it sounded like he had lost his mind.

The barn was built, then a few horses bought. Our daughter, Janelle, became interested in riding so an American Saddlebred mare, named "My Lovely," was purchased for her to ride and show in competition. She did well with Lovely, so a pleasure horse named Jack was added to the family. FLYING V FARM was born and for years we went to competitions all over the United States and Janelle was even invited to bring her horse to Paris for an exhibition during the famous race at Longchamp. We all had fun, but there comes a time when a decision must be made, and all the traveling around was taking a toll on my painting.

One Saturday morning in 1986, Vae and Gene Hamilton, who had recently moved to Conover, visited the farm and stayed most of the morning. Vae had been a horse lover all her life and was feeling the need to get involved again. We had a wonderful time, and it soon became obvious that she and I were two of a kind. She is also an artist, and we instantly became good friends. This friendship has endured for more than 30 years.

Shortly after, we began meeting other artists and eventually we became the group I dubbed "The Magnificent Seven" and later shortened that name to "The Mag Seven." Finally, we had: Kate Worm, Lissa Hamilton, Mary Dobbin, Bobbi Miller, Rebecca Warner, Vae, and me. These ladies were all art lovers, artists and/or writers and together we were awesome. Barnes and Noble Book Store eventually became our "headquarters" where we would meet and discuss art or what we were all working on and just be together. These meetings were frequent. One day as we were all leaving, we opened the wrong door and the noise of the bells and whistles from the security system and fire alarm scared everyone in the building. We were surprised we were allowed in the store again. Rebecca was the last to come into the group. She is a writer and has had five books published, some of which are on the Best Seller list. The neighborhood has never been the same with all of us loose.

Out of the blue one day, Kate called and suggested she, Vae, and I go to Chetola Lodge, Blowing Rock, North Carolina, in the mountains of our state, for a long weekend. She thought it would be a good idea to get together and share our thoughts about our work, our ideas for the future, where we were in our work, and what direction we wanted it to take. She also suggested we critique each other's work and discuss how to proceed. After that weekend we had a better understanding of our intentions. We decided to meet at least once a month to share ideas. Not long after that weekend Kate invited "The Piedmont Painters," a group of artists, to her home and included Vae and me. That's where we met Mary Dobbin. Mary was working on large, beautiful still life paintings with flowers, sometimes with fruit, and they were very nice. After a few years of being with our group Mary's family moved to New York due to her husband's job. While there she earned her master's degree in fine art at the Pratt Institute. We missed her and were happy when her family moved back to Lenoir, and she joined our group again. Unfortunately, we seldom get together now since we are all so busy with family and other things.

On July 18, 2001, Vae and Lissa taught a workshop on painting and writing at Appalachian

The Mags.
Vae Hamilton; your author; Rebecca Warner; Lissa Hamilton.

State University, in Boone, North Carolina. I attended and there were several others in the class. We had a great time. For years, I had kept journals on the various trips I had made. That class is when I realized that I loved to write about anything. Lissa gave me the tools I needed to begin, and so for the past 17 years I have written poetry, prose, and whatever subject interested me. Thanks, Lissa. You have made a difference in my life.

What can I say about Kate's work? She does beautiful, impressionistic paintings of people, and her abstract landscapes are gorgeous. Kate began painting about 40 years ago. Her formal education was in K – 12 in Basic Skills, Math, and Reading. She noticed that her four-year-old son seemed to have an artistic talent and wondered "where that came from." She was working at that time with aggressive teenage boys who were excluded from school because of their behavior. She had also published a natural foods cookbook with Prentice Hall.

She began to draw and paint in her spare time (hah) and discovered she was good in those endeavors. Eventually, she gave up working with troubled teens and started an advertising business with furniture manufacturers. At that time Hickory, North Carolina was one of the top regions in the country for producing furniture. In order to acquire a better foundation in art, she studied with Andrew Martin at UNC-G, Greensboro, North Carolina, for eight semesters, traveling there one evening a week.

Mary Dobbin; Lissa Hamilton; Pam Brock; Kate Worm; your author; Vae Hamilton.

Kate has always worked with the figure, and she also relates to landscapes, recently doing gorgeous abstracts. She said that two painters in the region have helped her immensely with abstract design, me, and Vae Hamilton. Kate says that good painting, whether realistic or non-objective, requires strong design and Vae and I have been inspirational and full of knowledge about those subjects. She also says my generosity knows no bounds, but that is true of most people. I do believe one must "pay it forward" and that's the best reward one can have. Helping other artists is important to me. Others have shared their talent, technique, and time with me, and it is necessary to "pass it on" when possible.

Kate, like the rest of the Mags, has traveled extensively, visiting many scenic areas of the USA, Ontario, Canada, and Europe, gathering information through on location painting. She says no place she has ever visited is as beautiful as where she lives in rural Alexander County, NC. I agree. I live in the middle of a large forest with all sorts of wild animals and beautiful scenery around that are excellent inspiration for a painter. My family has 14 acres of beautiful forest and our house is in the middle. We are located about about an hour from the large city of Charlotte, North Carolina and maybe 1½ hours from the mountains.

Kate said she continues to explore design elements within the context of realism and teaches painting at the Hickory Museum of Art in Hickory, North Carolina. Those classes are mostly on painting portraits with live models. Her portraits are awesome. Kate also offers 3 – 5 days gouache and watercolor painting workshops out of town. Over many years she has worked with people of all ages and abilities. One of the most enriching experiences for her has been with individuals at the Signature Studio in Morganton in Western North Carolina. She has mentored three adult painters with developmental disabilities at Signature Studios for 15 years. Now in her retired years she still paints and works as a volunteer instructor with the Hickory Museum of Art and in local churches. She also spends time with art activities and guiding her grandchildren.

Kate asked me to begin volunteering with her at the Signature Studios in an adjoining county. After just a few visits I realized that this is what art is all about. What those men taught me cannot be learned from a book or university class. Their attention span was remarkable for their disabilities, their interest complete and their compassion for each other incredible. I learned more from them then they ever did from me: compassion being the best.

One of the men, Brooks Yeomans, did a watercolor of me that he titled "Beautiful Lady." That small painting is a treasure and hangs in my studio today. I also have a much larger painting of a street scene that Brooks painted. These two talented men have exhibited their work in a gallery in Switzerland.

Kate's husband is retired now, so they travel a lot, visiting family and going places they have always wanted to visit. They also baby sit with their grandchildren when needed and love to do that. Kate still takes time to paint and sends work to galleries. I love to sit and talk to her. Recently, she came to my studio to study several books I have on the American Southwest. She and her husband were planning a trip there soon and they are interested in searching out the ancient pictographs and petroglyphs found throughout that region. While she was reading, I continued to paint on a large watercolor. It was like old times.

Kate is not the only one of us interested in the glyphs. Vae and I have taken two trips to the Southwest and our experiences were incredible. The first trip we made there together was exceptional. This was in September 2009. We had planned to roam around, paint when we could, take in all the sites and meet Bobbi Miller in Santa Fe, New Mexico for another week of traveling. Most people would think this was an easy plan to follow but considering that the two of us are so

Vae and Pat (your author). Two of a kind!

right brained most of the time we can barely function, problems did sneak into our plans.

The first thing we did when we arrived in Phoenix, Arizona, was rent a car and drive to Page, Arizona, reserve a room in a motel and prepare for a hike into Paria Canyon the next morning. After an early breakfast we drove to the canyon and stopped at the Ranger station for information and signed in to make the hike. The Ranger on duty was nice and told us the Rangers would be flying over the canyon in a helicopter several times a day, and if we needed help to wave a rag, towel, whatever we had so they could land and help us. Great. That's a good thing to know. He also warned us that in the event it began raining, we had to get out of the canyon immediately since the Paria River ran through it, and we would be walking in a dry riverbed that would become a raging torrent. He told us there might be a few spots with a little water but not many and during the time we spent in the canyon we saw none. The thing is, rain falling upriver from the canyon would affect where we would be hiking, so we must be always aware of the weather. In canyons there is nowhere for water go but up.

We went to the beginning of the trail, looked around a bit then began unloading our backpacks and lunch from the car. I had to go to the toilet and said to Vae, "Do not close the car door. I left the keys in it." She did not hear me. When I returned, she was standing waiting for me and I still had to get some things out of the car trunk, but it was locked, and the keys were inside. There was no one else around. We didn't know what to do. This was before cell phones and no one else

Bobbi's Painting

was there. After a short wait, the Ranger came by and called a locksmith in Flagstaff who would come, but it would be two hours before he would arrive. Fortunately, we had already taken our painting equipment from the car, so we found a place to paint and began working. Vae sat in the middle of the dry riverbed working away and I did a sketch of her painting and later did a large watercolor of her from the sketch.

When Sue and Bob arrived from Flagstaff to open the car, Bob worked for an hour and could not get the door open. We had lost an entire day by then and were desperate, so I picked up a big rock, knocked out the small, side window, and opened the door. However, the keys were not inside. We had to have the keys to open the trunk of the car to see if the keys were there. Bob removed the back seat and crawled into the trunk, found the keys then we had to pull him out. That episode cost $75, an entire day, a sunburn for Vae and me, but we made good sketches and learned a valuable lesson: Always know where the keys are before closing the door. And, despite the problem, we had a wonderful day in the canyon and have remained friends for many years.

The next day we finally began our hike through the canyon and had a wonderful time. The colors of the cliffs were beautiful, and the rippled grooves in the cliff made by water rushing through the canyon for centuries, were amazing. The hike we made took several hours and we saw only two other hikers during that time. We made it all the way to the Narrows before turning back. I think the Narrows is the halfway point and it was well named. In order to go through we would have had to take off our backpacks, one of us go through the narrow slot and the other hand the packs through. I have always wished we could have hiked the entire canyon, but Santa Fe and other interesting places were calling.

That night, at the motel, we met a family from China: A mom and her five children and the grandparents. Only the children's mother spoke a little English, but we managed with gestures, acting out our thoughts, and decided to have dinner together. We went to a nice restaurant, were seated at a large round table and chatted with each other with gestures and what few English words they knew. No one knew exactly what was said, but we all had fun and entertained everyone in the restaurant. When the waitress came to take our order, the grandfather spoke up and, pointing toward Vae and me and holding up two fingers, said, "Two Be-teks." He was ordering Beef Steaks for us. We both said, "No. No. We are vegetarians!" The five years old daughter whispered something to her mother and when we asked what she said, the mother answered, "She wants to know what you said, and I explained that you are both a vegetarian and that was like a dinosaur that eats leaves." Everyone in the restaurant was laughing at us. After dinner, they came to our room, and we partied until midnight. So much for a good night's sleep. It was adventures such as this that made our various trips so interesting and fulfilling.

Bobbi's Painting

The next day we drove to Chinle to visit Canyon de Chelly. It was Easter weekend and we planned to spend a day in the canyon. That afternoon we met a Navajo family who invited us to go with them to the Canyon Easter Sunday morning for an Easter Sunrise Service. How lucky can you get? It was an experience I will never forget. The weather was not bad, just a little chilly in the early morning air, but got warmer as the morning progressed.

There were not many people on the Canyon rim; mostly Native Americans with a few tourists. The Navajos were wrapped in the colorful blankets they are famous for creating and the tourists had on layers of clothing. There were a few residents of the area attending also. The morning was beautiful and clear: not a cloud in the sky. Two clerics, a Presbyterian minister read the Easter story from the Bible,

Chimayo Church.

while a Catholic priest, holding a small replica of an Anasazi bowl filled with damp cedar shavings he lit with a long stem match, walked throughout the congregation using an eagle feather to disperse the smoke to carry our thoughts and prayers to God. It was beautiful and moving, very spiritual and much appreciated by all.

The Navajo family who invited us to the Sunrise Service also asked us to join them in Albuquerque, New Mexico, the next weekend for the "Gathering of the Nations," an annual event where many tribes come together to worship, have dance competitions, demonstrations of bow and arrow making, and creating their tribal regalia. We had a few days before the Gathering, so we drove up to Santa Fe, New Mexico where we were to meet Bobbi Miller at the old bus station. She was joining us for a week of traveling.

When we arrived in Santa Fe, we picked Bobbi up at the station, enjoyed a day on the square, visiting with the locals, and shopping with the Native Americans who had their wares spread out on their colorful blankets. We bought a few trinkets, had a good meal (a taco salad) then drove to Ghost Ranch in Abiquiu where we would stay for two days seeing the sites there and getting acquainted with an Elder Hostel group who were studying dinosaurs. They were a fun group and we enjoyed being with them and learning more about dinosaurs from them.

During the night Bobbi became ill and spent most of the night running back and forth to the toilet. I was not far behind, but Vae was not ill at all. By morning we were okay but tired from lack of sleep. From Ghost Ranch, we went to Taos to visit my cousin, Donna Heinley, who owns an art gallery there: Heinley Fine Arts. Her gallery is where my paintings were exhibited, and I had a major exhibition of my work there. From Taos, we drove on the High Road from Espanola to Rancho de Taos. In Taos, we visited the beautiful 17th century adobe church, San Francisco de Assisi built 1813 – 1815 under the direction of the Franciscan Friar Jose Benato Perrera. The interior was beautiful, and the exterior striking, set into the landscape perfectly. It is an impressive landmark and famous. After a visit to Taos and my cousin, we headed once again to Albuquerque to attend the Gathering of the Nations with our new friends, the Navajo family. What a time we had.

We sat in the bleachers of the convention center with thousands of others. The dance competitions were the most interesting. We learned that each participant made his own regalia- (don't dare call it a costume)- and they were awesome and colorful. At one point, Bobbi, who can draw beautifully, was sketching the bustle of one of the dancers when he noticed what she was doing. He came running to her and was angry, saying, "Do not copy my bustle! I made it, and it is one of a kind." Bobbi apologized and did not continue drawing. The dancer did not know her drawing was just for her information and not to be reproduced. We were careful after that in choosing our subjects. We were not allowed to take photos of their regalia. However, we could take photos of the dances and other activities. Mostly we sketched and talked with the locals, enjoyed the different food stands and activities arranged by the Indians. It was an interesting, entertaining and educational experience.

After the Gathering, it was time to go home. We had spent 3 weeks traveling around, had a wonderful time, and enough memories to last forever. Our flight was without incident.

Another interesting trip Vae and I took was to Calgary, British Columbia, Canada, on August 18, 2002. Vae had attended a painting workshop at Springmaid Beach to study art for a week, working with Dr. Ernest Velardi, who taught at California State and is a purist artist. There she met Ursula Reynolds who told her about her workshop facility called River Rock. Ursula also told us that she was trying to get Dr. Velardi to teach a workshop in her art facility near Calgary, teaching the psychology of art. This would be one week of intense work for us and in a beautiful region of Canada. Vae had also been told about Dr. Velardi by Katherine Chang Liu, a well- known American artist. Dr. Velardi agreed. There was no way we were going to miss this opportunity. We were excited. Vae and I made our arrangements, gathered up supplies and left dogs and men behind.

Everyone who knows us knows that anytime the two of us go somewhere, we always have a happening, and this time was no exception. Our friend, Lissa Hamilton, took us to the airport.

Checking in for the flight was easy, and then we shared a plate of Chinese vegetables. We boarded our flight, taxied out to the runway, and waited, and waited, and waited to take off. We were finally taken back to the gate and told we would not be traveling that night. We got a new flight scheduled for the next day, and since we did not have a car to go home, we stayed in a motel close to the airport. In the morning, our flight to Dallas/Fortworth was on time and we left for Calgary early. What awaited us there? With the two of us you can never tell. But, of course, any trip with Vae would not be complete without a mishap or two.

When we arrived in Calgary and went to Customs, I was asked a few questions and passed through with no trouble. Not so with Vae. All her paints and mediums to be used during the workshop were confiscated. No explanation, no giving in: Nada. When she finally got through, and we rented a car, and we were given directions to two different art stores to try to find what she needed. Not much was available. We would be using liquid acrylic and tubes of watercolor. The only liquid acrylics available were small bottles. I told her I would share since I had plenty of paint in larger bottles. When we arrived at the studio and told the other participants what had happened, they too offered her some of theirs.

Vae's husband was notified of the confiscation, and he got in touch with the airline in Charlotte. They shipped the paints and other supplies back to Charlotte, then Gene drove to the airport and retrieved them.

First day, we saw geese, and all kinds of birds including hawks, before breakfast. There were three moose along side the Bow Valley parkway. On the car radio we were listening to info about the area we were visiting, and the broadcast was in French and that was a treat for me. There were more birds that day at Lake Louise: Clark's nuthatches, Forest Grouse, Black Bill Blackbirds, Western Red Tail Hawks and Ravens. We had a spectacular view of the glacier and lake. There were too many people.

The next morning the workshop began, and we got acquainted with the other participants and Dr. Ernest Velarde, the professor. I could tell from the beginning he was a special teacher. His lectures were informative, interesting and answered many questions for us. After 3 days, we had our first critique, and that's when I learned I do automatic writing in my paintings. I had not heard about that before and did not have a clue what it meant until he explained it to me. Never had anyone ever talked to me about my work the way Ernest did. I learned a lot about my use of color, the way I approached doing abstract and expressionist paintings, and why my feelings dictated the way I paint. He also told me to study the work of Cy Twombly who did automatic writing in his work.

After the workshop ended, Vae and I took a couple of days to visit Marble Canyon and saw some of the most beautiful waterfalls I had ever seen. The scenery in that region was varied and interesting, and we met lots of travelers. One of those travelers told us to be silent, look carefully, and we would see marmots. All we saw were many brown rocks. We were sitting at a picnic table, having a snack looking at the rocks when we suddenly realized those rocks had squinting eyes. They were not rocks at all: They were marmots, lots of them, and they were friendly and were waiting for a handout.

The next year, Vae and I went back to River Rock to attend Ernest's second workshop and had just as much fun and learned as much as we did the first time. That trip was different in that we were close to a forest fire, but it was contained, and we did not have to evacuate. At one point we looked out the window and saw all kinds of wild animals fleeing the fire. A gorgeous eagle landed on the railing of the porch, and we all took pictures of him. I never did a painting of him but did one of the deer family that passed by. Who says painting is dull.

Everything Professor Velardi told us about painting was new to us. The first morning, he began with a lecture about creativity that had been his lifelong study. He told us that the four phases of creativity are:

1.Preparation
2. Incubation
3. Illumination
4. Verification

He also said, "Incubation is the father of invention." He told us to prepare, envision, and work. All the things he taught us that week have been important and helped with my career as an artist.

Vae and I have shared many different experiences during the 30 years we have known each other. When we arrived home from the Southwestern experience, we were invited to have an exhibition in the Newton - Conover Auditorium Gallery in Newton North Carolina., featuring paintings we did from the Southwestern trip. One of my paintings was a large watercolor of Vae sitting in the middle of the dry riverbed in Paria Canyon. This was a complete surprise to her. She had not known I was working on that one. It is now hanging in her home. Some of the Southwestern paintings were large: French dyes on silk or collage. I love doing collages. Another exhibit we had together was at the Aiken Center for the Arts in Aiken, South Carolina. Later we exhibited together in the Rice Museum in Georgetown, South Carolina, and together taught a workshop there. Both of us have our work in that museum.

Vae and our friend Kichung Lee Lizee also taught a workshop together at Appalachian State University in Boone, North Carolina. Bridging the gap between Eastern and Western art was the focus of that workshop and it was interesting and informative. Kichung was interested in having us host Korean and Japanese artists for an exhibit in our museum and us doing the same with them in their countries. It all came about without a hitch and is discussed further in another chapter. It was fascinating to learn how to do the Oriental writing and we had fun with it. I have used it several different times in my work but must admit without a book on the language, I would never have had the nerve to try that. On arriving home, I found three four feet tall concrete drain tiles that were left over from a log cabin on my property. The cabin had burned. I had them placed in the flower garden, painted them scarlet red, and painted on them three words in Chinese Calligraphy. Those words read THE WAY, HAPPINESS, and TRANQUILITY. They are in my yard, and visitors always want to know what the Chinese writing means. Every year I repaint them, so they are always fresh. These columns began life as drains from my family's log cabin that had burned. They were all that survived. The ultimate re-cycling.

In the past few years Vae has been very occupied with her art, concentrating on birds and horses and pets. She and Gene purchased a place in Florida and spend most of the winter there now. She returns to their home here in North Carolina frequently to ride her horse, Cloud, and visit with friends.

Rebecca is our writer with five published books to her credit. She and her husband live in Asheville, North Carolina, now, having sold their large home in the mountains of North Carolina. She also paints some, and I have one of her small collages. We don't get to see her often, but it is always a fun time to be with her, and we talk on the phone. Like the rest of us, Rebecca's interests lie in many directions. We met in the summer of 2001, but in September of that year her mother had her third open heart surgery, so Rebecca went back to Florida to take care of her for six months. Her mother passed away April 1, 2002.

After that, for the next 5 years, she took care of her father through a series of illnesses including a broken hip, after moving him to North Carolina. He passed away in 2011.

Despite these situations, Rebecca has managed to get five books published, the first one in May 2014, the second released in October 2014. Her third in August 2015 and was selected for inclusion in a romantic anthology along with nine other authors. It did very well and reached the *USA Today Best Seller List*. She also wrote for the *Huffington Post* for two years after getting involved with politics in 2016.

Rebecca and her husband, Jason, have been to Europe eight times since we met in 2001. They also took Jason's sister and her husband to Venice in 2001 when she and Jason renewed their wedding vows for their 25th Anniversary. Rebecca has added so much to our group of terrific women.

Our friend Bobbi and I have chatted by phone a lot lately, and she is helping me remember some of the activities we all shared. She and her husband, John, live in Wyoming. We hope they will be moving back here soon. Bobbi is one of the featured artists of the Jackson Hole Land Trust, working in a 60-page sketchbook and doing oil paintings representing the four seasons at a designated Wyoming ranch, which features captivating scenery. We recently had a long conversation about the reproduction of the pictographs and petroglyphs of the Southwest. A Navajo artist with whom I became acquainted told me that the Indians believe it is a sacrilege to copy them exactly, but I don't know if that is the belief of all Indian Nations or just the Navajo. I never use them in my work unless I can make them up and that is difficult to do since there are literally thousands of them throughout the Southwest, and they are etched forever in my memory.

In 2000, Bobbi and her husband, John, purchased property in Wyoming, and the western landscape became part of her family's journey. John had become enamored of that area before their move there, having hunted and fished in this state for many years. He convinced Bobbi to look around for "that little cabin in the woods." One thing led to another, and the log cabin became a full-time home in Moran, a town named after the famous 19th Century artist, Thomas Moran.

After hyperventilating about leaving friends in North Carolina, she acquiesced to moving full time to the wilderness. Of course, an adjustment was necessary, but as we all know, when "one door closes, another opens," and new friends were made, specifically through an outstanding arts community in neighboring Jackson Hole.

Bobbi now happily embraces the solitude of "America's Serengeti" while becoming engaged with the fine arts in the Jackson Hole area. Jackson Hole is one of the premier art communities in the US and Bobbi has participated by forming the "Teton Plein Air Painters," engaged in plein air events at the National Museum of Wildlife Arts, with the Jackson Hole Land Trusts and continually attends programs at the JH Art Association.

Snow shoeing, cross country skiing, and hiking have been added to their recreational repertoire. Bobbi continues to connect by visiting friends in North Carolina and underscoring art groups in Wyoming. Of course, family is most important, and their three grandsons receive much attention.

Another interesting thing about living in Moran is that their Internet does not work very well. They go into to Jackson frequently for visits to doctors, dentists, better Internet and some entertainment.

Naturally, their friends hope that one day they will return "home," and we can all pick up where we left off. And we hope that soon we can have a Mag reunion.

We are all so busy with our lives now that it is hard to find time to be together. We met for lunch recently and that gave us all a chance to catch up with each other's happenings and vowed to continue getting together monthly when possible. These women are special and important to each other, and we must continue to stay in touch.

And now I must tell you that my beautiful, talented friend Mona "Vae" Cunningham Hamilton passed away on October 3, 2022 after battling Leukemia for more than a year. I will always remember her for the fun things we did together, the trips we took, the compassion she had for all living things the forty years of friendship we shared, her love for her family and friends, and the constant smile she always had on her beautiful face. Goodbye my friend. I will see you soon.

Your author and Vae Hamilton

SOUTHWESTERN SOJOURN

Arriving at the airport in Santa Fe, New Mexico, with my friend, Vae Hamilton, who was traveling with me, and we picked up a pre-ordered rental car and began our three-week experience in the Southwest. We drove to Taos and immediately checked into a local motel and began planning what we would see and do in the time we had allocated for that area. In less than a week, we would go back to the Santa Fe airport to meet our friend, Bobbi Miller, who would be joining us for the remainder of our trip.

Vae and petroglyphs.

Taos, New Mexico. Oh my. What a gorgeous little town of about 7000 people, full of beautiful adobe buildings that are famous. The town is also well known for its numerous art galleries, rich history and those distinct adobe buildings, one of which is the Taos Pueblo. The Pueblo is a collection of multi-storied adobe dwellings that have been inhabited for more than a thousand years. It is the only Pueblo in the Southwest that is designated a UNESCO World Heritage site and is also a National Historic Landmark. I was fascinated by its history, beauty, and age. Taos also has the famous Harward Museum of Art, second oldest art museum in New Mexico. Their collection includes Hispanic works and visual arts from the Taos Society of Artists, Taos

Moderns, and contemporary art.

Vae and I have traveled together several times. We were looking forward to seeing all the interesting places in and around Taos and learning about its history. Before this trip I had no idea it would be so interesting. One of the first places we visited was the gorgeous San Francisco De Assis Church in Rancho de Taos. It is an ancient adobe building and looks as if could withstand a nuclear attack. Beautiful.

After visiting the gorgeous church, there was much to see and do in and around Taos: Hiking, hot air balloon rides (no, we didn't take one), winter skiing, and beautiful parks. There is also the incredible Rio Grande Gorge Bridge crossing over the Rio Grande River. It is 650 feet above

Taos Pueblo Church.

the river and the views of the landscape from the bridge are spectacular. From that area you can explore the rugged landscape in the Rio Grande del Norte National Monument. When Vae and I had done all that, we spent time in the Historic Taos Plaza in the heart of the town. The Plaza has everything you could possibly want: art galleries, shops, live music, and we could watch people to our hearts' content. There were also many displays of the regions culture and heritage.

The local Native Americans had arranged their handmade wares on colorful blankets all around the square. Their silver jewelry was beautiful, and each vendor was different. They all used colored semi-precious stones and approached the mountings in different ways. I bought a lovely silver feather shaped necklace with five different colored semi-precious stones of different size and shape down the center. The silver chain was simple but beautiful, and I have worn it many times and received lots of compliments. There were colorful baskets of every kind with beautiful designs, and they were gorgeous. The pottery was exceptional, and I truly wanted one but couldn't figure out how to keep it safe during the remainder of our trip and on the plane ride home.

After this visit, doing all that, and having so much fun we left to go back to Santa Fe and pick up our friend from home, Bobbi Miller, at the airport. Bobbi has a story too. Her husband is a big game hunter and went to Wyoming often to hunt. As I mentioned, a few years ago, they left North Carolina and moved to Wyoming. Bobbi is a wonderful artist and has become

Taos Pueblo, New Mexico.

involved with various art groups where they live. They recently bought a home in Florida and spend winters there. After picking her up at the airport in Santa Fe we went to Abiquiu to spend the night at Ghost Ranch and see various things in that area. Recently we had a long telephone conversation with the other Mag 7s about the fun we had on that trip. We laughed and reminisced for nearly an hour.

Ghost Ranch. Oh my. In the past Ghost Ranch operated as a dude ranch: A destination for visitors and tourists. Georgia O'Keefe, a famous artist, arrived there in 1937, but the owner, Arthur Pack, had no room for her. He suggested she stay in Rancho de los Burros, a short distance away. She was immediately attracted to the site, purchased 12 acres on the edge of

Ghost Ranch, built her home and lived there for 40 years. Smart lady. Georgia O'Keefe has been called "The Mother of American Modernism." It is no wonder that she is world famous for her beautiful paintings.

During our first night there, Bobbi and I fell ill and spent the entire night taking turns running back and forth to the toilet. Vae did not have the same problem but did not get much sleep. By morning we were okay so we left that area to continue our trip. The remainder of our Southwestern visit was spent painting on location around that area for few days then went to Abiquiu and loved that area too. There was something interesting around each curve and lots of

Bryce Canyon hoodoos.

trails off the highway to explore. The scenery was spectacular in that area and we took advantage of the time we had to see as much as we could.

Our next stop was Paria Canyon where we hoped to see the fabled sunlight piercing the slot canyon. Our Native American guide explained to us that the canyon would be wonderful in spite of the overcast sky. He guided us into the slot canyon, where we would see the incredible sandstone cliffs with unbelievable patterns formed by centuries of rushing water. In the canyon we saw the slot canyon and were told that during certain times of the day the sun would penetrate the slot and make a gorgeous display of a light beam inside the opening. Vae, Bobbi, and I, along with our guide, stayed in the canyon longer than we had planned, so we could see the beam of light, and not once did the fabled shaft of light come in. The sky was full of huge cloud formations

El Santuario de Taos.

that blocked the sun.

The remainder of our Southwestern visit there was spent painting on location around that area for a few days then we went to other areas until we had to return to the airport to fly home. It was a fun time and we did lots of work. Our flight home was uneventful and I was happy to get back to work in my studio.

"It is 6:30 a.m. and I am sitting on the rim of Bryce Canyon in Utah, waiting for the sun to come up. The ghostly figures of the hoodoos loom below me like creeping beings from outer space. Very slowly a faint pink glow appears on the horizon, illuminating the rim. The pink intensifies and slowly the tops of the hoodoos turn a pinkish gold. My eyes are glued to the different rock formations in anticipation of the coming spectacular. The light creeps across the surface. Suddenly the sun pops up above the horizon and the panoramic view of the amphitheater of gorgeous rock formations comes alive with dancing light, creating a scene yet to be copied by man. The formations straight ahead are backlit and look as if there is a light deep within making them appear almost transparent: an ethereal light I had never seen before. How beautiful. How mysterious. How wonderful that I, in my solitude, can look upon such a sight and be filled with the Spirit of this place and of the ones who came before. I am blessed."

The above was taken from a journal I kept while on a nine day trip through Utah and Arizona with an artist friend, Neil Crandall. Neil's occupation is a restorer of fine art. That's how I met him. He restored a small, over 100 years old watercolor by Francis Hopkinson Smith for me. I had bought the painting for a small amount, had no idea who the artist was or how much it was worth.

Several years later, while flipping through an art magazine I saw a similar one by the same artist. I bought the magazine and read about the artist and his work. I was blown away by the information. I knew immediately the painting needed to be in our museum for others to enjoy. Our Hickory Museum of Art specializes in American art and I knew they would be thrilled to have the painting in their collection, since they did not have one of this artist or his father who painted in much the same way. Recently the painting was on display in the library of the museum and I really enjoyed visiting with it.

When Neil and I arrived in Phoenix it was hot, 105° F and even the dryness did not help. When it is hot, it is hot! We had a terrific adventure driving the Apache Trail going 22 miles on a dusty, unimproved road with not a drop of water in sight. When I was there with Vae, it had been raining, it was cool and there was a waterfall.

Once again, I'm here in Antelope Canyon, Page, Arizona and this trip is more awesome than before because the weather is different. This time the sun was shining, and the beam of sunlight penetrated the slot at the time it should, not once, but twice. It was an awesome sight. I took several photos and hoped to do a painting of the scene when I returned home. I eventually did

San Francisco de Assisi Church, Taos, New Mexico.

paint the scene and the painting sold during one of my exhibitions. Unfortunately, when I began searching my photos for the one of the sunlight in the slot canyon, it was nowhere to be found. I wish I had kept the painting. We did not want to leave but Bryce Canyon and the North Rim of the Grand Canyon were calling.

We wanted to make a few stops at other interesting places like the Best Friends Animal Sanctuary located in Kanab, Utah. However, by the time we arrived there it was closed and we were disappointed. We were lucky to find two rooms for the night at Ruby's Inn, the last two rooms available. Early the next morning, we drove to Bryce Canyon. I was not prepared for the beauty of the place and felt as if I was in church. The sheer beauty of that canyon inspires deep emotions to surface and everyone there was whispering. All I could hear was the chirping of the birds, the chattering of the squirrels, and the whisper of the gentle wind in the trees. We sat on the hoodoos (rock formations) and waited for the sun to come up. The hoodoos in front of us slowly came alive with the rising of the sun and became almost transparent. The beautiful sandstone glows with a soft inner light even when the sun is not behind them. In reflected light the hoodoos have an aura. Nothing can compare to the vastness and beauty of that massive hole in the ground. It was a wonderful experience that will remain in my memory forever. Later that day we drove to the Grand Canyon.

Beautiful Navajon pots; watercolor.

The drive into the canyon was heartbreaking. Two years before a forest fire had devasted thousands of acres of pine and aspen trees. The skeletons of the burned trees are a reminder we must always be diligent in keeping our natural resources safe. But the beautiful day shed an incredible light, making dense shadows on the colorful display of "mountains rising out of the depths." How anyone can hike into that canyon and back out the same day is a mystery to me, yet it is done frequently in good weather. I stood in awe of that beautiful place. I seemed to hear voices from the past telling stories of the events that had occurred there during the past centuries.

I didn't want to leave but the road was calling.

Our next stop was Cottonwood, Arizona, where we planned to visit my artist friends, Jim Scott and Ted Schmitt. It was a good visit, and we caught up with what had been going on with us since our last meeting. Seeing the work Jim had been doing since he retired to live there was proof he had made the right move. His watercolors are gorgeous. I could tell he felt perfectly at home living in the Cottonwood area. We went to dinner in a nice restaurant, found a motel and the next morning we drove to Sedona. It was difficult to leave Jim and Ted after such a short visit. I had the feeling Ted would not be with us much longer.

It was time to head for Sedona where I would do a lecture-demonstration of my collage painting technique for the Northern Arizona Watercolor society. The lecture-demo was titled "*Getting Outside Your Box*." The group was very nice and made me feel welcome, especially the president and the program chairman. I feel I made lots of friends there.

The lecture-demo went well, and I finished a painting during the allotted hour. I had brought several paintings in various stages of completion in case I could not finish the demonstration. The attendees had a good time looking through them. Before beginning to work on a clean surface I gave them a good dose of Professor Ernest Velardi's psychology of painting, which they seemed to enjoy. Using bits and pieces of paper and silk fabric that I had previously painted and brought with me, I began collaging on a very smooth synthetic paper called Yupo that does not buckle. This technique was much easier than using a canvas or canvas board which would be difficult to travel with. While the collaged pieces were drying, I talked about collage and how much fun it was to take bits and pieces and make something beautiful. At home it sometimes takes hours for a painting to dry, but in the dry desert heat the collage dried in minutes and that made it easier. One artist commented that my hands were flying over the painting. Their response was excellent, and I felt that I had done a good job. The finished painting was okay. I named it "A Day with Southwestern Artists." They loved it. The enthusiasm of the group was worth the trip out. They were asking questions right and left.

Deer Dancer.
Nambe Pueblo watercolor.

Not only did I have fun doing the demo, but spending time with good friends of long standing, in their home, was a special treat. Being with Gretchen and Chuck in their beautiful home perched on the side of a mountain was a visit

I had enjoyed before. Gretchen's sister attended the demo and said she was exhausted trying to paint along with me. Another artist said she was tired of painting the same old way and could hardly wait to "GET OUTSIDE HER BOX". Bingo.

That evening, Jim and Ted came to dinner with Gretchen, Chuck, Neil and me. We had a wonderful time reminiscing about all the times we had been together, the trips we made, and the camaraderie we shared, and with other friends who attended Jim's painting workshops. Jim and I had painted together many times on various trips and he taught workshops. I could write another book about the workshops he had sponsored over many years. Once I arranged for him to exhibit in our local museum and give a watercolor painting workshop. It was an excellent exhibition, well attended and also lucrative for Jim. Many local artists attended the workshop, had a wonderful time and really enjoyed Jim's humor, teaching ability, and dedication

I hated to leave but it was time to head back to Phoenix and take our flight home. On the way we stopped at the Deer Valley Rock Museum and Trail Park. There we met Desert Little Bear, a Native American who was a volunteer guide that day. Little Bear had good stories to tell us about the area and he was also an artist. We talked about art and what it means to us. Suddenly I looked at him and said, "You understand, don't you?" His answer was, "Yes. And you were born art." He asked if I had photos of my work, so I showed him the few I had with me, representative of what I do. He had donated several pieces of his work to the museum and Neil bought one for my birthday.

Little Bear's work is very different from mine. He searches on the Reservation for flat or slightly rounded talus covered stones (Desert Varnish), then carves petroglyphs on them. The one Neil bought for me is named "The Maze of Man." It is beautiful and when I look at it, I can feel myself going back into the canyons and mysterious places where I searched for and found so many glyphs over the years. The native Americans believe it is a sacrilege to copy the glyphs exactly, so they make them up. Perhaps that is why, even though I had never heard that legend, I painted over a large triptych of the Thompson Springs pictograph panel that is 5,000 – 9,000 BCE years old. I simply did not feel good about copying it. The panel on the cliff wall is named The Holy Ghost and His Family. Meeting Little Bear was an unexcepted experience and I learned a lot about the Navajo Nation.

It was time to go home to get ready for my niece's wedding, and there would still not be time to paint. Changes were in order. When painting sessions get few and far between, little Patty Sunshine turns into a real.... well, Stinker.

Not long after the trip, Gretchen, my friend, passed away. That was quite a blow to me. She was a talented artist, wonderful woman and a good friend. Soon after, Ted died and then two years later, Jim passed away, and I was devastated. He was such a good friend and inspiration to

Expressionist painting of adobe wall by Viles.

me and many others. I was heartbroken to lose three of the best friends I had ever had. They impacted my life in many ways and I will be forever grateful for having had them in my life. I will always remember the fun times we had together.

Sunday Morning!
Different churches along the high road between Santa Fe and Taos, New Mexicao.
French dyes on silk by Pat Viles.

Poppy field near Taos, New Mexico Ink on silk by Viles.

Mountain Scenery, New Mexico. French dye on Silk by Viles.

Vermillion Cliffs National Monument,
Paria Canyon, Utah.
French dye on silk by Viles.

Memories of the southwest. French dye on silk by Viles.

Petroglyphs of Utah.

Parawan Gap. Capital Reef Park.

Strangers slipping
Quietly through the night,
Traveling through,
looking for a place
to tell their story.
In the distance,
they see a cliff,
smooth, gleaming
in the faint light of dawn.
They write their message:
"We were here."

The Great Gallery, Horseshoe Canyon, Canyonlands Park, Utah.

CHANCE ENCOUNTERS

Sometimes fate steps in and suddenly you meet someone who will become very important in your life on many levels. I have been fortunate enough to have that happen to me numerous times. The first was my teacher when I was 12 years old. The second was a young man, Ardle Lee Viles, who became my husband and life partner for 40 years. More about him later.

Another was James Godwin Scott, an artist from St. Louis, Missouri, with whom I shared more than 30 years of friendship before his death in 2016. In 1987, I saw an ad in the American artist Magazine where he was teaching a watercolor workshop in Sault Ste. Marie, Canada. After talking with my husband, I called Jim to see if he had space for my Canadian friend, Barbara, and me in the group for the two weeks workshop. The conversation went something like this:

"Jim Scott speaking. How may I help you?"

My reply was,"Hi. My name is Pat Viles from North Carolina, and I read your ad in *American Artist* about your workshop in Canada. Would you have space for my Canadian friend, Barbara and me?"

Jim said,"Why honey, I thought you would never call."

I knew immediately that this was going to be a very interesting, entertaining, and special experience. Barbara and I had met in a language and art school in Avignon, France, became friends, and I called to tell her about the workshop. She loved the idea and was thrilled that attending was possible. I flew to the American side of Sault Ste Marie, rented a car, got directions to Stokely Creek Lodge and drove, and drove for what seemed like hours, deeper and deeper into the forest, finally finding the place late in the afternoon. It was gorgeous. It was surrounded by dense forest, lots of flowers growing and not another building in sight. Even though the sun was shining there was lots of shade and it was cool. Well, it was Canada.

On meeting Jim Scott that evening before dinner, I address him as Mr. Scott and he said, "Drop the mister crap. My name is Jim." I never made that mistake again. The other members of the group were very friendly and we liked them immediately. They told us they were all from St. Louis, Missouri. Barb and I were the only "foreigners" in the group. It was a bit daunting to be the odd gals out, but we should not have worried. Everyone was friendly and happy to have us join them. The group was about equal men and women and had different levels of painting ability. Barb and I fit right in.

The next morning, after a great breakfast, we went on location to the first painting site Jim had selected. He proceeded to do a beautiful demonstration of the forest then we all began to paint. This was the first workshop I had ever attended outside of my home state of North Carolina and the first time I had ever actually painted on location. I had no idea how difficult it would be with the sun moving around, the wind blowing, and mosquitoes as big as hummingbirds biting us. Thank goodness I had brought a long-sleeved sweater and a large bottle of bug spray.

Everything was green. I thought I would never be able to do a painting with mostly one color in it but Jim explained to us how to look and see the different shades of green, and how they were changed by the sun and shade. We painted until noon, picnicked, then continued working throughout the afternoon. That first day was awesome. I managed to paint a decent watercolor before going back to the Lodge.

After a couple of days, Barbara and I were completely comfortable with the others. Since there was nowhere to go after the work of the day we gathered in the common room and began talking about our day and how much fun it had been. There was no TV but a table full of games and a piano. That was not a problem since we had so much to talk about of our day. One of our group played the piano so we listened to his "concert" then sang songs together. It was a fun filled evening. Eventually, we began telling stories about people we had met, and how they had influenced us in different ways. Then someone recalled what one of the group had said or done that day. We were all laughing and having fun telling stories about some of the silly things we had done. Then Jim said, "I am so glad I don't have any funny characteristics." During his demo that morning he had turned to us and told the story about being in a workshop with Georgia O'Keefe. She had turned toward the group, pointed her paint brush toward them and said "I live on the edge of a knife." At some point during his demo that day Jim did the same thing. He turned toward us, threw out his arm with paintbrush in hand and said, "I live on the edge of a knife."

That evening, after dinner we were all sitting around the fireplace talking about the day and how much fun it had been. We exchanged stories about silly things we had done or said, and everyone had a story. Jim laughed and said again, "I am so glad I don't have any funny characteristics." Not knowing if Jim was a good sport, I stood, picked up a pencil, and copying his St. Louis accent, turned toward the piano and acted as though I was painting and lecturing, then turned to the group, threw out my arm with the pencil and said, "I live on the edge of a knife." The group laughed hysterically and he said, "OMG. I have become a character." Yes, Jim was a good sport and definitely a character. From that day on until he passed away in 2016, he was a wonderful friend and supporter of mine. He was like a brother to me and I loved him dearly and so did my family and friends who met him when he visited my home.

One day during the two weeks we decided to go to Hurst, a village that is the last outpost of civilization in that part of Canada. In order to get there, we had to take a train. When I was driving in to the Lodge, I never saw any evidence of a train rail, train car or station so I wondered where we would meet the train. We got in our cars and drove to a parking area in the woods. Surprise. Surprise. There was train rail there. After a few minutes we heard the train whistle in the distance. The train came roaring in, stopped, and we got on.

On the trip we saw nothing but forest. Once in a while the train would stop and people would appear out of the forest, unload one of the cars and then we would move on. At one stop a rail car was detached from the train and left there. Several people appeared out of the forest and began unloading the car. We were beginning to wonder where in the world we were going. There was a party car so for the 3 hours trip we had a good time with the rest of the passengers and crew. By the time we got to Hurst, half the people were slightly inebriated and hungry. We would have three hours to look around and eat lunch. The only restaurant in town had a limited menu, but it was sufficient for us. We ate together then spent the remainder of the time looking in the shops and talking with the locals. There was snow on the ground even though it was autumn, but the locals were still out and about and I enjoyed talking with a few of them. They had interesting stories to tell. I found one shop that had Eskimo dolls made by a local artist. The dolls wore typical Eskimo winter clothing made by the artist from real fur, beads, and heavy thread. Beautiful. I bought one for my daughter.

When the time came for the train to go back through the forest, we were surprised that it had not turned around. We were going to go backwards all the way through the forest to where our cars were parked. On the way back the train stopped at places again to leave off supplies they had picked up in Hurst. When we got to the place where the rail car had been left, it was reattached to the train, and we continued our trip. It was a wonderful and completely unexpected experience. Soon after that experience it was time to return home. We reluctantly said goodbye to each other not knowing that in the future some of us would be together again with Jim in other workshops.

This was the beginning of my friendship with Jim and many more like-minded people. We had many wonderful trips together when Jim organized workshops in different places. A lot of that original group would go and many others from all over the States would join us. Since I was able to speak French, we had several trips to France, visiting areas with which I was very familiar. Some of the places were the same ones my friend Maggie and I had visited on our trip to paint in Monet's Gardens, when, in 1992, we received a grant from *Reader's Digest* to paint in the Gardens. We added 6 weeks to the two we would be painting in the Garden, and during that trip, we covered most of France. I knew Jim would love those places so we visited a lot of them and had a great time. The participants all became friends of mine. Those were great fun times. Over the years the countries we visited to paint, besides France, were Spain, Switzerland, England, Greece, Portugal, Madeira, Ireland, and Bermuda. I, alone part of the time or with my husband, visited Norway, Denmark, Sweden, the Netherlands, Costa Rica, and other places in

Jim's class in St. Etienne de Baigorry, France.

Jim, Pat, Ted, and friend.

Central and South America.

It is really different traveling with a group after going with Maggie part of the time with my husband on occasion or when I was alone. Being alone and being able to speak French, I made lots of friends and had experiences most people don't have when traveling in a foreign country and when I went with Jim we did connect with my friends when possible. It made the trip more interesting when we could interact with the locals and my ability to speak the language was very helpful. But, we were not so lucky in the countries where none of us spoke the language. Even those times were wonderful, funny and in some cases life changing.

Ireland was a real treat for all of us and was a beautiful country. Jim and his life partner, Ted, took painting groups to Ireland three times, staying in a small hotel in the village of Ballyferriter and using that village as our base, painted at Slea Head on the Ring of Kerry, Clogher Beach, in many of the small villages and had a wonderful time.

The Irish people were very friendly and welcoming. They would tell us about good places to paint and how to find them, and occasionally, someone would take the time to lead us there. Maggie and I went there twice, and I went with Jim and his workshop painters three times.

Before Maggie and I went the first time to France, she came to visit me when I was at our vacation house on Seabrook Island. Walking on the beach one afternoon we met a couple from Northern Ireland who invited us to visit them when we came to Ireland. The next time we went to Ireland, we called them and got directions to their home. The drive along the shore in Northern Ireland where they lived was spectacular. The scenery was beautiful with rugged cliffs, interesting rock formations and the gorgeous blue-green water. The waves were very high that day and sounded like thunder. The sound of the pounding surf made conversation difficult. This visit was during the time that Northern and Southern Ireland were at odds but we had no trouble at all. It was a truly wonderful visit. We spent a few days with them and painted all over the area where they lived.

I have been so fortunate to have Maggie in my life, and friends all over the USA, Europe, Canada, China, Japan and Korea. They have all enriched my life dramatically. I AM THE LUCKIEST WOMAN IN THE WORLD.

During our travels together Maggie was always buying souvenirs and storing them in her backpack. When we arrived back in New York from the first Irish trip and went through customs, I realized she had left her sketchbooks in the cart on the incoming side of customs. She went running back toward the gate waving her arms in the air and yelling, "As God is my witness, I will never buy souvenirs again." The customs officials actually allowed her to go back through and retrieve her sketch books and come back to meet me. Her sketchbooks are beautiful, a constant reminder to her of the fabulous trip we took together to Ireland, and are irreplaceable. To my knowledge she has never "shopped" again on a trip. It was a miracle the books were still in the cart. It would have been a disaster if they had not still been where she left them. Maggie is a master watercolorist and those books were irreplaceable.

After Maggie and I stopped traveling together so much and I became acquainted with Jim Scott, I began going on painting workshops with Jim. Those trips were always excellent and it was fun to be with Jim and his workshop group. One of the most interesting places Jim took a group was Switzerland, to the small village in Iseltwald, perched on the side of a small mountain. My family had friends who owned an excellent chalet located in the tiny village of Iseltwald on the banks of the small Lake Brienzerzee. The collection of homes in the villages were all built on the banks of the lake. We stayed in the chalet owned by my family's friends. The chalet had been turned into a place for groups, mainly religious, and was offered to us by the family who owned the chalet. We went there twice. It was a very beautiful, quiet place and we enjoyed it and the wonderful meals prepared for us.

The chalet overlooked the lake and every day we would take the ferry or a bus to our chosen painting site. Priscilla, my friend and whose family owned the chalet, had a cute little black dog named Blackie who was well known by everyone on the lake. Blackie had a collar that held a little barrel that opened and inside was his ferry ticket. Most mornings Blackie would go to the nearest dock and get on the ferry. The ticket taker would open the barrel, take out the ticket, and punch it, then return it to Blackie's little barrel. Blackie would make the rounds of all the stops, visiting his friends, and if he happened to miss the last ferry of the day, someone would call Priscilla and tell her Blackie would be spending the night.

Blackie, the traveling pooch!

From the chalet we would go to different places to paint each day, one of which was Wengen, perched on the top of a huge mountain. Wengen is famous for its ski slopes and there were always hundreds of people there. From the parking area we took a cable car to the top of the mountain that overlooked the valley and the distant mountain range, the Three Sisters: the Monck, the Yungfrau, and the Matterhorn. How beautiful they were. Covered with snow, deep shadows, and no discernable trails, I wondered how anyone could ever climb those peaks. They were simply awesome. It was always crowded there and sometime it was difficult to find a place to sit and work, but we were all so engrossed in our work when we did settle down, no one bothered us.

Finally, we found a good place and Jim did a beautiful, full sheet watercolor color demonstration. After that we all spread out and began painting. I chose a place where there were few people and began working. I was totally oblivious to what was going on around me when suddenly a booming voice said, "Pat. Your painting is beautiful." I jumped, knocked over my easel, splashing water on the painting, ruining it. It was Jim, but I won't repeat what I said to him. Behind him about 30 people were sitting on the rocks watching me work, and I had not known they were there. They were completely quiet and respectful. When the accident happened, I got a standing ovation at my remark to Jim. They, Jim, and I were all laughing. So the moment turned into fun event even though the painting was ruined. Jim gave me his just finished painting that day. I got the best end of that happening.

Another beautiful place we visited was the Chateau de Chillon. It was very cold that day and our water and watercolors were freezing. I wondered if the freezing colors and water would help us paint the cold. And that might have worked except our water and paint kept freezing. We were spread out over a large area of the lawn and had just begun to paint when a large man came from a storage area driving a huge mower and began driving over the grass. He was actually blowing off the snow and we were in the way. He never yielded to us and we were scrambling to get out of his way. That's a real trick when you are balancing an easel, palette, backpack, water bucket and a huge portfolio full of paintings and watercolor paper. After an hour we were able to get back to work, but we wondered why he chose that particular time to begin blowing with all the many people all around and the artists working.

There were so many interesting places to choose from it was difficult to make a decision. The next venue we chose was the Valle Maggia, on the border of Switzerland and Italy where Lake Maggiori was located. Our bus took us there and we chose places along the road that gave us a wonderful view of the lake and surrounding landscape. We had been told the road was not heavily traveled that time of the year. Everyone chose a spot and set up their easel to begin. We were painting away when we heard a loud, clacking sound that sounded like a helicopter. It was a helicopter and it landed in the middle of the road where we were sitting on the sides, blowing over our easels, paper, palettes that went flying through the air. Our hats and scarves were also blown away and our jackets soaked from the water buckets spilling on us. We finally collected our things and set up to work further away. Later we learned the

The Parthanon, Athens, Greece.

Ruins in Greece.

helicopter was ferrying building supplies to the top of the mountain and that explained the stacks of lumber close by where we had been painting. Who says painting is boring? Every trip we made had an "experience" that was different, sometimes a bit dangerous and always funny. Thank God for laughter.

In 2007, Jim and his life partner, Ted, came to visit my husband and me. I had arranged an exhibition of his work at our local museum that specialized in American art. After the opening reception Jim, Ted and I drove to Seabrook Island, South Carolina, close to Charleston, where my family had a beach house. We planned to stay at least two weeks and paint all over the coastal area. One day we went to a large pond not far from the house, planning to paint all afternoon.

Jim chose his spot and I pointed out to him the flat space down the bank near the water and said to him, "DO NOT go down the bank to the flat area because our ponds have alligators in them and they sun themselves there." There was no comment from Jim. Ted and I went further down the road to another area and began working.

When I finished, I walked back to see how Jim was doing and saw that he was standing within inches of the water, on the flat surface, and directly behind him was an alligator about 6 feet long. I didn't panic. Calmly and quietly, I said, "Jim, please, very slowly go around in back of your easel and ease up the bank. There is an alligator a few feet behind you." He leaped about 5 feet onto the bank and ran like the wind and I could not catch up with him. When he finally stopped, I said, "Jim, I had no idea you could move that fast." His reply was, "When you look death in the face, you run like the Hants of Hell are after you." In the incident, his easel went flying into the lagoon, and his new 15-page pad of expensive Windsor Newton watercolor paper also flew into the lagoon, and his easel was bent. I assumed that, since the alligator did not attack Jim, he had already eaten his breakfast.

That was the first day. The next day we went into Charleston to get him more paper and a new easel. He fell in love with Charleston so we planned a daylong visit to paint there, since there was no time to paint that day we shopped. When we did go back, he painted like a fiend and was like a mad man rushing around from one place to another, getting more and more "turned on". We spent a few more days in the city as well as painting in several interesting areas nearby. We all really enjoyed the beautiful, historical plantations in that region before returning to my home in North Carolina.

Our experience in Greece was wonderful too. Athens was a metropolis with houses built in every nook and cranny like every city. We stayed a couple of days then took a ferry to the island of Crete. The city of Heraklion was beautiful from the dock. Houses were everywhere and the city was not as industrialized as I expected. It is the home of the 4000 year old ancient city of Knossos. The light there is incredible, perhaps because there were no factories in the city proper

Fresco in Candia Museum with copy in the old area.

so the air was more pure than you would expect. The people were friendly, and I was excited about going back to Knossos to once again visit the Minoan Heritage site. The first time I visited, I had an unusual, very emotional experience written about in another chapter. Later on I joined a group from Rutgers University for an educational tour there. It was excellent, and the professor gave some wonderful lectures.

Knossos was built by the Minoan Civilization 4000 years ago, and it was fascinating. Some of the ruins have been restored, and it was interesting to learn that 4000 years ago, they had running water and flush toilets. The original frescoes had been removed and taken to the sixth floor of the Candia Museum where they are now displayed and reproductions were put where the originals used to be. The frescoes were beautifully copied and made to look as if they had been there 4000 years, even to the fading of the colors. They depicted scenes of the people's daily lives, and what was said to be the Queen's bathroom had a gorgeous fresco of dolphins and fish swimming. One of the frescoes had a tree with a blue monkey swinging from a branch. That was really interesting because I was told there are no monkeys in Greece. We spent lot of time in the museum learning about the Minoan civilization. The original frescoes were absolutely beautiful. I was totally fascinated by them. How could they still so beautiful, vibrant with color, after so many centuries?

After our visit to Heraklion, we took a ferry to the spectacular island of Santorini. I could live there. The homes are built one after another, all connected by pathways and steps, painted white, and the houses had beautiful bright blue roofs, shutters, and doors. They are on the side of a sheer cliff that descends to the beautiful azure blue water of the Aegean Sea. Gorgeous. Steps lead down to the edge of the cliffs, the houses are very small, and all day, you can see burros and small horses loaded with building supplies and other commodities going up and down the steps delivering things to the different work sites. Not once did I see a pile of excrement or urine on the beautiful white steps. How the steps and houses are kept so clean with all those creatures going up and down them is a mystery. They look as if they are freshly painted every few days.

At a later time, I went back to Greece with the Rutgers University group. We went by bus to visit many other Minoan ruins around the entire island of Crete. To this day, I am totally fascinated by this civilization and have done many paintings one of which was 11 feet wide and 9 ½ feet tall folding screen for a client to put in the new house he and his wife had built. The screen had scenes from six different 4000 year old frescoes from Knossos. He and his wife have bought several other paintings of mine, some of which were done on my trips to Greece. Another painting I did that I liked very much is a collage of a scene on the Island of Santorini, and it hangs in my house today. Standing on one end of the island and looking toward the village of Ios, you can see the most spectacular sunset imaginable. One night, we had dinner there and watched the sun sinking slowly into the Agean sea, throwing beautiful colors over the island. It was amazing.

Another chance encounter came about when I listed my work with an art group from Canada, Painter's Keys. My website was featured along with others and shortly after that I received an email from Carl Schlademan, an artist from Saskatchewan, Canada. Carl had seen my work on the internet and wrote that he liked it very much and was impressed that there was not a barn or haystack in sight. We began emailing, and even though we have never met in person, through photos we have become friends, critiquing each other's work and encouraging our endeavors. We talk on the phone frequently. Carl's work is very different from mine. His paintings are nearly always very large and impressionistic. His paintings of sunsets are absolutely gorgeous, and I envy his ability to capture such beauty. He also does beautiful photography and sends me photos of scenes from his Province in Canada. My work is mostly expressionistic or abstract, very colorful and fairly large also. I do like to do small paintings, though, to give as gifts and for hanging in smaller spaces. Smaller paintings are great for hanging in groups. I treasure the friendship Carl and I have developed over the years and hope someday we can finally meet in person.

The adventures I had with Maggie and Jim and others were wonderful and gave me memories to last a lifetime. The friends I made, the things I learned, places I saw and things we did were exceptional and are seldom enjoyed by most people. What a treat it was to find so many people who thought, acted and enjoyed life the way I do. I am grateful.

Being with Maggie and Jim has always been an interesting and exceptional event for me. They are both scatterbrained and lovable and a lot of fun to be with. But there have been others who are important to me in different ways.

My friend, Joanne Wilfong, who I have known for several years, has recently become more like a sister. 2018 has been one for the books for both of us. On September 13, 2018, I had major surgery on my neck. This caused many problems for me, not the least of which was months of recovery. Then, in March 2019, I fell while feeding the deer and broke my hip and that required a complete hip replacement. Joann became my confidant, chauffeur, kept me grounded, brought me flowers, telephoned every day, and was simply "there for me." I got better, began to drive, and her support continued.

One day she called and said, "You are not going to believe this. I fell in the yard and broke my knee cap, have a soft, full leg cast and can't drive." Whoops. The tide had turned and it was my turn to become her confidant, chauffeur (driving her car since she could not get into my van), keep her grounded, take her cookies, telephone every day, and simply be "there for her". Joanne was also dealing with the illness of her daughter, Laura, who has cancer. Laura is now in remission and doing great. We are living proof that good things can come from bad situations. Thank you, Joann for everything.

There have been many chance encounters in my life that have been wonderful and meant a lot to me. Now I have become more active in our local museum that is a fantastic one, residing in what used to be the old Claremont High School. It is now a huge complex called The SALT Block: Science, Art (and aquarium), Library, and Theater filling one entire block of the city. Over several years I have had more than one solo exhibitions of my paintings with the last one being a retrospective covering 20 years of work in 2016. While I still paint, my claim to fame there now is mostly for the cookies and other goodies I make for various occasions. The museum also has three of my paintings in their collection.

In 2017, our director, Lise Swenson, retired and Jon Carfagno came to the museum as director and has done a tremendous job and we hope he will stay forever. Over a period of about 5 years, Jon has worked miracles with the museum and it is now one of the best in the "Southern States" and we are so happy to have him and hope he will stay forever. He was responsible for us having a blockbuster exhibition of the work of the famous artist Andy Warhol in our museum for three months. Every day for the length of the exhibit the museum was full of people. The parking lot was always full and the car licenses were from many different counties in our state. Jon and his remarkable staff have turned our what used to be a small-town museum into a blockbuster one. Whoopee. Hickory, North Carolina and its wonderful museum are now on the map.

KINDRED SPIRITS

Two lovable pests!

There are no accidents! I have proven that to myself over and over during the many years I have traveled to paint and learn about other countries, their customs, language, the people and how to get along with others who are really not so different in many ways than us Americans.

I believe that what we do with our lives is preordained and if we listen to our "inner voice" (our Spirit Guide) and absorb the messages it gives us we won't go wrong. When I finish my time on earth I want to be sure that I have left no stone unturned, no doors unopened, no chances let slip away, no lessons unlearned and have had many, many wonderful experiences learning about other people from other countries, their customs and their languages. I want to have had wonderful experiences with many people who became mentors and friends. I don't want to have lived a quiet life of never getting outside my box. If I have been an inspiration to just one person I will have been successful!

As I said in the beginning there are no accidents, so when I returned home from a three months long, intensive study of the French language at the Institute de Francais, a language school in Ville Franche Sur Mer, a village near Nice, France, my husband was away on a two week business trip in Chicago and I would be alone. For me that was not a problem. There was laundry to do from the trip, mail to open, and a mountain of newspapers he had saved for me. I tackled the latest editions of the newspapers first and right away saw a small article about a watercolor workshop in Lancaster, South Carolina, a small town not very far from my home. It was to begin the next day. The instructor was Margaret Hall Hoybach, an artist who lived close to Charleston, S.C. I thought about it a few minutes, called and learned there was a space for me, signed up and prepared to drive to Lancaster late that afternoon.

The next morning I met the teacher and other participants and began a fun weekend. It took me about five minutes to know that Maggie was special and we would become good friends. We knew almost immediately we were KINDRED SPIRITS and this was the beginning of a 30

Pat and Maggie's exhibit together in France.

year friendship! We knew we would stay in touch. During the three days of the workshop, I learned that Maggie was a lover of Impressionist painting and was inspired by the work, philosophy, and palette of Claude Monet. There were several other artists in the group, and we had a wonderful time together. Everyone did a lot of work and had good paintings to take home. I learned a lot from Maggie, and we became friends.

On returning home a few days later, I bought groceries, and while checking out, saw a *Reader's Digest* magazine and on the cover (be still my heart) was an article about Monet's Garden in Giverny, France! I bought it and before I put the groceries away, read the article. *Reader's Digest* had undertaken to help finance the restoration of the Giverny property, restoring the house and gardens to their former glory and was offering a grant for qualified artists to spend two weeks painting in the gardens! After thinking about it a few minutes, I called Maggie to tell her about the grant. The conversation went something like this:

"Monet? Giverny? Paint? OMG! Yes! Yes! Yes! When do we leave?"

I replied, "Settle down, Maggie, we have to know the requirements, when, how, etc. before we could be accepted. I will call the listed phone number to learn what the requirements are."

After she calmed down, she agreed. We talked a few more minutes, then I said I would call her back after I had the information. I made myself a cup of tea, sat down with the telephone in front of me, gathering courage to make the call. Finally I dialed the number and talked to a very nice lady who told me we needed to send 5 examples of our work, write an essay on why we wanted to go, choose a date and send it in as soon as possible. I called Maggie, told her the requirements and she overnighted the info to me. I immediately sent the information, and a few days later I received a call saying we were the first artists chosen to paint in Monet's Gardens!

I called Maggie with the news, and she freaked out! It took a while for her to settle down. We talked a few minutes, then I suggested that we add a week or two to the trip and paint as much as we could. After thinking it over, we decided two weeks were not enough, so we settled on two months for the entire trip and that would give us six weeks to paint in other areas of France! We talked about the trip for a while, deciding what our intentions were and began planning so we could take full advantage of the time we would be in France. We could go anywhere we wanted to since at that time I was fairly fluent in French and we would get along just fine!

We began our trip in the Pays Basque Region of France, staying in the tiny village of St. Etienne- de-Baigorry that is situated only a few kilometers from the border of Spain! We flew into Biarritz, picked up a previously ordered rental car and had our first "experience" a few miles down the road! We nearly ran out of gas! I had never been in that area before, and this was in 1992. We did not have GPS or cell phones, and it was Sunday. We finally found an open service station and pulled in with the car running on fumes, filled up, and started out again. Little did we know that our two months in France would be filled with experiences that would be talked about for years and that we had not planned on or expected to have.

Maggie and Pat's Art Gallery in France.

We drove into the tiny but very beautiful village of St. Etienne de Baigorry and easily found the small Hotel Arcé owned by the Arcé family. We were shown several rooms, chose the one we wanted, and not once did they ask for an ID, credit card: nothing. We were amazed! We had chosen a room overlooking the rushing Nest River that ran through the village. The patio, built out of stone, was situated on the bank of the river and was only about two feet above the river with no barrier between it and the rushing water! Across the river was the main part of the town. The weather was perfect. When we walked out the front door we could see the Roman Bridge that the villagers used to cross the river from the town side. Everywhere we looked was a paint-

Near St. Etienne de Baigorry.

Roman bridge over the Nest River in St. Etienne.

ing. Maggie was bouncing all over the place and couldn't wait to get started painting but the car had to be unloaded, we had to make plans to best use the time we had there (a week, maybe more) and ask for suggestions from the Arcé family as to the best places to go.

So, we took a load of "stuff" to the room, and I went back out to get another load. When I got back to the room, Maggie had unloaded a bunch of her art supplies and her clothes and they were all over the room including my side! Since I had never traveled with her before, I was totally unprepared for her being such a lousy housekeeper! I dug into my backpack, found a piece of chalk, pushed all her things to her side of the room, drew a chalk line down the center and told her NOT to mess up my side again! We had a good laugh, and that was the only problem we had during the entire two month trip. AMAZING!

What can I say about the Basque Region? There were mountains all around, yet we were only about 40 kilometers from the sea. From the hotel we could go about 12 kilometers to a steep road that led to Spain. From Biarritz it was only a few miles to many interesting places and very close to Italy. We didn't know what to do first and finally decided Spain could wait until the next trip. Dinner that night was superb: Basque vegetable soup, fish and truffles meuniere, beef tournedos and asparagus, all delicious and beautifully presented. Being nearly starved we cleaned our plates and afterward sketched from the windows and the patio. Maggie was in heaven, and I was more interested in talking with people, getting my French pronunciation back and hoping it was fluent enough to get us by for the next few weeks. The France we were in and would be during the entire trip required the language, as we wanted to stay in the less traveled areas, off the beaten track. Maggie was fascinated at how friendly the people were and how they wanted to help us. It was a fantastic beginning to what would be an experience we would never forget and I loved speaking the language I had worked so hard to learn, but there was a bit of a problem! I am from the Southern state of North Carolina and have a bit of a Southern Accent to my voice. It took a few days to overcome the problem, but I never got to the point of acquiring the proper French accent! However, it did improve over time thanks to the patience of the French people helping me! They appreciated my having taken the time to learn their beautiful language!

Every day was a different experience. We would go into a restaurant and on the menu would be Soupe de Garbure and it was always different. After a few days I asked one of the waitresses why it was always different but had the same name. She laughed and said, "It is made with whatever is left over from the day before." We began calling it Garbage Soup and when we went into a restaurant where we were recognized, the waitress would yell out "Deux Soupe de Garbage va arriver!

Translation: Two Garbage Soups coming up!

So, during our first week we were introduced to a family who had owned the hotel for many years, painted sheep, mountains, flowers, people, sketched from the Roman Bridge, and learned a bit about health care. Maggie got sick and a doctor was called. He came to the hotel. The visit went something like this, (in French of course, since he spoke no English): "Does this hurt?" Maggie groaned, and I said "Oui! (Yes!). "Does this hurt?" "Non". After a complete examination he decided she had a kidney infection, gave her some medicine and a prescription to take with us and told me to take her to another doctor in about a week to be sure she was okay. He knew we were traveling. In fact, everyone in the village knew about us and they were always friendly and helpful.

St. Etienne and the area around it were gorgeous. Flowers everywhere, the river flowing outside our hotel, the weather perfect and Maggie was painting like a demon! Her sketchbooks are priceless! She would complete a beautiful watercolor sketch in minutes whereas I would labor on a full sheet watercolor paper for an hour. Finally, I got smart and began painting in my sketchbook also, but I simply could not get onto the small format the feelings about what I was seeing and at the end of the six weeks, I had very little to show for it except hundreds of photos, more memories that I could count, and my French getting better and better.

One of the most interesting encounters we had was the result of seeing a sign at the end of a curving road that read "Atelier," which means "studio." The path was sandy and narrow and led to a large house surrounded by flowering fruit trees. We met Patriz, the artist who shared the house with his mother. From his tiny studio, Patriz does beautiful little pin and ink sketches and then adds watercolor. He is also a sculptor. Maggie and I could not resist acquiring his work so we both bought a small one and mine hangs in my home today. He was not aware of an excellent brand of watercolor paper we used so we each gave him a full sheet of Arches 140 lb cold pressed paper. That was interesting since the Arches paper is made in France! Patriz was very appreciative and thanked us profusely. Neither he nor his Mother spoke English, but we had a nice visit. Thank God for Le Professeur Kuropas who hung with me for nearly three years during my French studies at our local Lenoir-Rhyne University!

Further down the path was a cemetery with very old Basque carvings on the crosses. Home seems even further away than usual since we are in a region of France that most Americans never see, speaking with people who don't speak English and being only minutes from Spain and Italy. It was very hard to take in all the beauty of the mountains, the rushing river, the flowers, birds singing, the sky so blue and the clouds so white and nearly impossible for me to get back to trying to record it all on paper! Each day was wonderful, and we were sad to leave our new friends, and the fantastic hotel Arcé where we were treated like family during our visit. But, other adventures awaited us, so, off we went into the unknown! Don't tell Maggie that I went back there several times with James Godwin Scott and his workshop group. Yep! I was the interpreter!

The food specialties of the region were fantastic, and we indulged as much as we could. This part of France is different than others. It is the Basque Region and borders the Basque Region of Spain. Fortunately for us, there were no problems between the two countries while we were there, as there had been in the past. The wooly sheep, the river, the flowers, the Roman Bridge, were different from those we had at home and the people there were simply wonderful to us. We hated to leave but there were other interesting places to visit, more experiences to share so we packed the car and drove off into the noon sun, so excited about what was ahead, and drove to Tarbes where we would visit with my friends, whose daughter had spent a summer with my family the year before, along with a young man from France and a boy and girl from Spain. All were teenagers.

The Gaubert family was the epitome of hosts! Dinner that night was a feast! Madame Gaubert is an excellent chef and we were excited to have such a wonderful home cooked meal! We were sad to leave the next morning, but the snow-covered mountains of the Haute Pyrénées were calling. The Gauberts offered us their chalet at La Mongie and we accepted gratefully. The trip up the mountain was a feast for our eyes. There was a gray stone church nestled at the foot of the mountain and there was, once again, wooly sheep looking for lunch. Our lunch consisted of a petite quiche picked up at a patisserie and eaten beside a swiftly flowing brook in the shade of apple trees in bloom. Maggie and I sat on rocks in the middle of the stream, sketching and listening to the sounds of the wind, the rushing water, the song of the birds and the silence was profound at times. It was magical! After sketching a bit we could not resist having a snowball fight since there was plenty of ammunition left over from a recent snow storm; this without a coat! Little did we know that from then on we would be involved in another adventure with which we were totally unprepared to deal.

Easter Sunday. Carmelite Convent.

And then it was onward and upward until we finally reached La Mongie at nightfall. Starving, we looked around and only a small pizza parlor was open and was about to close. Madame made us a pizza and asked where we were going and then told us there was a blizzard blowing in during the night. Since we had nothing in the way of food except a few dried up prunes and all stores were closed, she was concerned. The ski complex was closed for the season and the only person there besides us would be the concierge of the chalet complex. Madame was closing the pizza place for the duration of the storm, so she gave us a basket of her left over veggies and we proceeded to find our unit and settle in for the night, not knowing we would be held captive the next morning by at least 3 to 4 feet of a late Spring snow! We existed for 3 days on little food, no vistas to paint, just killing time until we could break out and continue on.

The second morning, we heard a scratching at the door. We opened it and found a St. Ber-

Pat painting on the way to Castang.

nard dog, viewed only through about 10 inches of space between the top of the door and the snow! Maggie stood talking to him while I frantically searched for a dishcloth and pen to write a note to tie to his collar hoping the dog's owner would find it. There was no brandy or food attached to his collar and I did not find anything large enough to use, no pen, and no telephone number to call for help! In the meantime my Tarbes friends, the owners of the chalet, contacted the concierge of the complex who agreed to take us down the mountain in his jeep. Our friends had insisted we come to them until the storm was over. Down we went, speeding around hairpin curves, slipping and sliding, wondering if we would get out of this alive.

So we went from famine to feasting on gourmet food prepared by Madame, were shown the beautiful city of Tarbes, dined in a gourmet restaurant and, once again, enjoyed the friendliness and hospitality of the French people. Two days later Alain, Madame's husband, and a friend of his who had a four wheel drive, bought a set of chains, drove to La Mongie, dug our car out of the snow, put on the chains and Alain then drove it back to their home for us! He even had the car cleaned! Once again a wonderful family had taken us in and made us one of their own, treating us to an outpouring of love. My love for the French people and their country was, one more time, strengthened and will always remain for me one of the highlights of a completely wonderful trip that few Americans ever have the chance to enjoy.

The Gaubert family is indeed an international one! Madame spoke French, Spanish and German, Alain spoke French and Spanish, Stephanie, the daughter, spoke English, French and Spanish, I spoke English, French and a smattering of Spanish, Maggie spoke English, German and some Spanish, so for the first time she could be included in the conversation and we both felt wrapped in a blanket of love by people who barely knew us.

The highlight was a visit to a Carmelite Convent to attend an Easter Mass. This Convent is cloistered so the nuns seldom become involved with others. The Cathedral was located near Lourdes. The service was incredible with the priest speaking in both English and French! Being cloistered, the nuns were behind a gorgeous, shiny brass gate that separated them from the congregation, the Altar, and there was only a small opening through which the Priest administered the Sacrament of Holy Communion to them. Sunlight was shining in through the windows, over the congregation, causing bursts of light dancing off the brass and highlighting the white habits of the Nuns and Priest. It was a beautiful service and even though I am not Catholic the service meant a lot to me and gave me sense of peace I had not felt for a long time. Not being Catholic I could not take Communion, so I crossed my hands cross my chest and received a blessing instead.

One of the nuns was elderly, obviously not well, and was physically supported by the others. Their voices blended beautifully in singing a hymn that was beautiful and inspiring. I did not want to leave the church! After the service, one of the nuns and the priest greeted the parishioners at the door. I could hardly wait to paint my memory of the event but, with regret, the next morning we left the Gaubert's, wending our way forward to another adventure!

What did the future hold for us? The answer was not long in arriving! Descending the mountains through gently rolling hills, farmland, and green pastures we went north on our way to Castang, our next abode, Chez Guittard, a gite (bed and breakfast) we found in our guide book. Once again, we were back in the starving mode since it was Easter weekend, nothing is open and the gas gauge on the car says we are close to being stranded and we are lost. The only clue we had was our Guidebook listing the gite we had selected to stay in for a few days.

Finally, arriving at our destination, we found, once again, a little bit of French paradise, the small farm with four small houses, a barn and other small outbuildings, all overlooking scenery so beautiful it could make an artist cry! Again, we are in a part of France most tourists never see! At this point in time I am so wrapped up in the memories of our first two weeks in France I can't believe there could be more exciting things to come our way for the next month. Once again, I was wrong! Oh my! If I had only taken time to reflect on former visits I had made to the families of other students my family had fostered during summer vacations from school, I would not have been surprised. Those families gave me a true picture of how family life is in France and certainly is not much different than our own.

Maggie painting on the way to Castang.

Our experiences visiting the Guitard farm were just as impressive as the one in St. Etienne, except we were to live in a stone building attached to the main farm house and we would have a kitchen with a stove, fire-

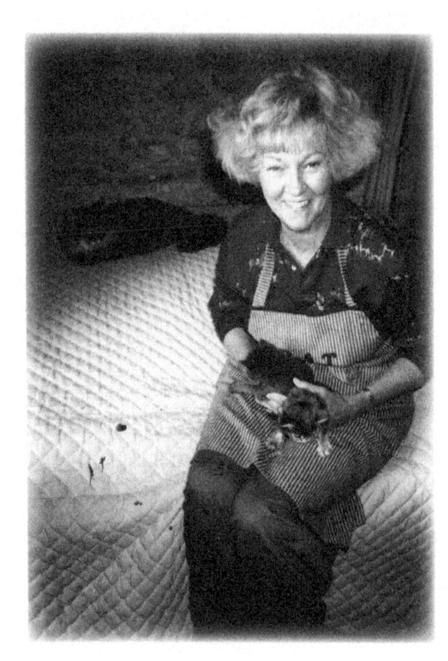

Pat and Pamplouf's kitten.

place, refrigerator and no food. This meant a trip back to town in search of an open market or food store. After three hours of searching in vain, we realized this was a "mission impossible" and returned once again to old bread, water, old prunes and painting. Everywhere we looked there was a painting to be done! Beautiful scenery, old stone buildings, gently rolling hills, and open spaces: a real feast for our eyes.

There was one bathroom to accommodate the people living in the six available rooms! The room that had been reserved for us was tiny and had a three-quarter bed for both Maggie and me! Since I had called to make the reservation, I had to wonder if my French was really as good as I thought it was! For whatever the reason, we were relegated to sleeping together that night and looking for a larger place the next morning. We were exhausted, so we decided to retire early. Now, neither Maggie or I are very large but a three-quarter bed did not allow much room for turning over and certainly not tossing and turning. Around 4 am. Maggie had to go the ladies room. We had a flashlight, but she didn't want to go alone since it was at the end of a long hallway. The very old house had squeaky floors, so everyone in the house could hear the sounds of our moving around. When we got back into bed, we lay there for a few minutes and then Maggie said,"I think in the morning we will have to upgrade to half a star!" We had a good laugh and made the best of the situation.

The next morning, Madame Guitard served a great breakfast of porridge, bread, jam, butter and cheese, and, of course, coffee, all by the fireside. It was a feast and welcomed, since we were starving. She told us everyone else was leaving, and we could move into the family room where we would have a table and chairs, closet, three beds, and complete privacy and be much closer to the ladies room, which turned out to be a blessing. It was also the closest to the barn where the "largest and loudest mooing cow in the world" lived!

Once again we were the recipients of French kindness when Madame brought a beautiful bouquet of flowers for Maggie to paint since she had learned in the short time we had been there that flowers were Maggie's favorite subjects. Later that morning, Maggie took a walk around the farm and come upon a house where a cat and lovely lady of the house were sitting in a window. Maggie was invited in, met Monique, the lady. She was introduced to a basket full of kittens the cat, Pamplouf, had just birthed. Monique's house was typical of most French rural houses with a large fireplace, copper pots hanging on the wall, vases of flowers everywhere, in the two rooms of the tiny house! The bedroom was very small, had a large four-poster bed covered with handmade quilts and tapestries lying around, and the basket with Pamplouf's 6 kittens was on the bed. Monique spoke fluent English and was an English teacher in the local school but would only speak French with me! What a way to begin another adventure!

The Guitard farm is a real working farm complete with farm animals and so different from any place we had visited so far. After looking around, seeing the light, shadows, animals, people and buildings, Maggie said, "It is no wonder that art is the national pastime for the French!" I had to agree.

During the first stop of our trip in the Bosque country, Maggie had fallen ill with a kidney infection, seen by a doctor and treated with medication. I was told to take her to another doctor, in a week to be sure she was better. I asked Madame Guitard which doctor I should take her to and she made an appointment for us and told us where to find him. Her directions were simple: You will see the doctor's office next door to the fire station on Highway so and so. Great! We started out, found the proper highway, and drove and drove and drove up and down! There was no fire station to be found. As I was driving down the highway, Maggie said, "Gee, I am glad I'm not having a baby!" After quite a long time we finally stopped and asked directions to the doctor's office, only to learn that the reason we had not located it before was the old fire station had been torn down and the new one built in another area. Madame Guitard was not aware of the change. Sure enough, the doctor's office was next door to the empty lot where the fire station once sat and since it did not have a large enough sign to see from the highway, we could not find it. Maggie did need another round of the antibiotic but not immediately so we continued our stay in the rural part of France, painted and had a wonderful visit.

The Flower Vendor

But the time came to move on so we began another segment of our journey toward the Massif Central with Limoges as our destination that day. Many years before this trip, my family had hosted Nicole, a teacher of English in a private school in her town. Nicole and Pierre, her husband, live in Panazol, a suburb of Limoges. On an earlier trip I visited them and they introduced me to Sarlat, an ancient village of pre-historic caves, one of which was Lascaux, and pictographs that are thousands of years old. It was there that my fascination with ancient writings and

The Fishing Boat.

pre-history began and continues to this day. Once again I would be transported back in time and Maggie fell in love with the place.

Close by the caves is the village of Rocamadour, a medieval village with buildings carved out of the sheer cliffs. From there we wound our way through limestone hills overlooking the Algon Valley, on a very narrow street only two to three people could traverse at one time. From the castle ramparts, we could overlook the village, staring in wonder at the basilica that keeps watch over the incredible village below. It was hard to leave this beautiful, ancient place! But leave we must since Limoges and friends are awaiting our arrival.

Once again, I would be in the company of Nicole and Pierre Morange at their home in Panazol, near Limoges. They welcomed Maggie and told us of a few plans they had made. They took us on a visit to the Bernadeau Porcelain Factory where Maggie purchased a beautiful piece of blue and white Porcelain to take home. Nicole took us to a local artist studio, a man who worked in enamels that were beautiful. I purchased three very small, exquisite, enamels he had done of drawings his three children had made. They are hanging in my home today! Maggie had been purchasing blue pottery, tablecloths, etc., to take home and I began to wonder how she was going to get all that "stuff" in her backpack. We have at least another month to go!

Back on the road, we realize we have a long way to go before arriving at our next destination

Ladies of the Red Hat Club!
Pat wears the Red Hat!

and we are hungry with no market in sight. So what else is new? It is then we began to realize that being hungry is a necessary part of this journey. What is a little hunger compared to the adventures we were having? When we were with Nicole and Pierre, they took us to a gourmet restaurant, Au Moulin de la Gorce, a three star restaurant and the memories of the delicious food we had there makes our hunger more painful!

Our destination that day was a tiny coastal village where we would spend the night and depart the next morning for the Atlantic island of Ile d'Yeu, where no cars are allowed. We would spend the day there painting, but first was ----FOOD! That night we feasted on Galatea of Crepes and Ratatouille. Hoping for a good night's sleep, we found a place to stay but getting a good sleep was a dream that never came true! The biggest and loudest trucks in France passed by our window, honking horns, changing gears, and it never stopped all night, making sleep impossible! It seems that lack of sleep and starvation go hand in hand on this trip but who cares? We were still having the time of our lives! In the morning we began preparations to take the ferry to Ile d'Yeu so we had a quick breakfast and then packed our gear once more for another adventure.

It was time to get Maggie's antibiotic prescription filled so, while I checked out of the hotel and stood in line to buy ferry tickets, I told her to go to the pharmacy, hand the prescription to the pharmacist so he could fill it for her. When she arrived, there a lot of people were waiting. When it was finally her turn, the pharmacist began a torrent of French, and, of course, Maggie could not understand a word. Using a mixture of English, French, and Spanish, she said, "Un moment, yo tengo an amie who habla Francais muy bien!" Everyone in the pharmacy laughed and someone finally told her the pharmacist had to get the medicine from another place and she would have it before the ferry left! We had a good laugh over that!

And so another adventure began. We got on the ferry for the one and a half hour trip to the island and Maggie immediately got motion sickness from the large waves caused by a storm off shore. Poor thing! She was miserable and mostly just sat there without talking to anyone. On the ferry was a French family who was traveling with their dog, Dick. They were chattering away and it was good for me to hear another French dialect. I could understand okay, but it took concentration since their dialect was pronounced differently from the French I had studied.

On arrival, Maggie was feeling better, and we were excited at all the things going on. Lots of people milling around, shops full of interesting things, and so many wonderful subjects to paint. We didn't know where to begin. Everywhere we looked, there were plenty of subjects. The beach, boats with flags flying, active surf, people walking, children playing, outdoor cafes full of people having a great time, all of which lent a festive feel to the place that would continue through the evening. We left the village to walk on the beach and throughout the residential area looking for a less crowded place to paint, and finally just gave up, found a spot, and began working, which drew lots of people asking questions about who we were, what we were doing, where we were from, and my French got quite a workout. Not once did we see another American, further proof we were in a part of France most tourists never see.

Maggie zeroed in on a stark white wall with a gorgeous, flowering vine growing on it and proceeded to paint a small masterpiece in her sketchbook. I painted the ocean and a nice boat moored close by. It was a wonderful morning and we enjoyed every minute of it. We took a short break for lunch, feasting on local seafood and people watching, while we sneaked in a few sketches. The atmosphere was alive with laughter, color, noise, boats coming and going; a real holiday feeling was evident. But all good things must come to an end so we reluctantly packed our things and embarked on the ferry ride back to the mainland, tired but very happy.

Maggie, Pat, and the de Guerville Family.

On the return trip, the same family and their dog, Dick, were with us and Maggie quietly began sketching them, finally asking their permission and we spent most of the trip talking with them while Maggie sketched. The French are famous for taking their dogs everywhere with them. This won a lot of brownie points for me because, when possible, I take both my dogs everywhere. Fortunately, Maggie was not ill on the return trip. The family was very nice and kind to two total strangers and once again, we made friends and discovered we had a lot in common.

So another adventure began, and we continued North toward Nantes where we visited more

Michelle's flower arrangement. Watercolor by Viles.

friends of mine. On this major highway we pass through the area of Vendee. We stopped for a picnic and painted the 17th C Moulin de Vent (windmill) and then on the road again, no stopping until we arrived at the home of the Huet de Guerville's. Robert and Michelle are longtime friends of mine, two of their children having spent summers with my family. I had visited them many times and they have visited my family along with the Sachets, from Paris, where we met in New York, and then toured the New England countryside. I knew Maggie was in for a real treat! She was totally unprepared to be welcomed like a long lost relative, so, once again, she found love and warmth and nothing of the expected detachment she had been told was indicative of the French people!

Michelle prepared a real feast for us with a typically French meal consisting of fresh salmon, white asparagus, fresh picked strawberries, and appropriate wines. The entire family of five children, their husbands, grandchildren, etc., were there to greet us. It was a raucous crowd, laughing, remembering our other times together, and telling the family about our experiences enjoyed on this trip. For me, it was like coming home! Since the children spoke some English, Maggie was once again included in the conversation.

The next morning, before we left for Brelidy, they took us on a tour of Nantes to see the beautiful Jardin des Plantes. The black tulips and orange azaleas were spectacular! Maggie was sorry to leave such beauty that would make a gorgeous painting. We took lots of photos so I am sure she did some paintings from that garden later.

Another lasting experience I had with the de Guerville family was during an earlier trip to visit them. One of their daughters was getting married and my husband and I attended the wedding. The year before when I was with them I was brought into the Ladies of the Hats Club, which meant in order to be a part of the group I had to wear a hat! So, having a small head, it took several hat shops to find one that fit me and it was bright red! So I bought a red hat in a shop named the "Red Hat Shop" on Red Hat Street! Then I had to find an appropriate outfit since the one I had intended to wear did not go with the red hat and that is another story! Find one we did, and the wedding and reception were beautiful. The dinner afterward at a local hotel was spectacular, and many glasses were raised in toast to the happy couple. They now have four children.

I was sad to leave my good friends, but the time for returning home was getting closer, and we had much more to see and do! And once again, we were on the road, this time to visit the fabled land of King Arthur in Normandy. We must not tarry! We were expected at the Chateau Hotel de Brelidy where we would stay in the 16th century chateau. This chateau had been restored to its former beauty, updated and is now a very, very nice destination for travelers. It is owned by Eliane and Alain Yoncourt, and we were looking forward to meeting them and learn more about that area of France. We knew Eliane was fluent in English, and Maggie was excited about that!

The red tiled roofs and white houses we had enjoyed so much were left behind and replaced with sturdy stone houses, sparsely placed, and with few trees. Everywhere there was evidence of the wars that had been fought during many centuries. The Chateau was situated on a hill overlooking the valley and old bunkers from World War II could be seen all around. The chapel, outside the Chateau wall is still used today. Serenity abounds here but I wondered how the people can remain so serene with all the evidence of so much war all around. It is amazing that the French people are still capable of being at peace. Their resilience is remarkable. I stood be-

Maggie and Anna.

side the chapel, looking out over the peaceful landscape, and began to see a veil parting, giving me a glimpse of the past and a hope for the future. How lucky Maggie and I are to have such an opportunity of traveling, painting and getting to know a people who are becoming more and more important to us as we continue on toward the artists' Mecca: GIVERNY!

I am so wrapped up in all the things we have done, the people we have met, the work we have accomplished, that I wonder how much more my mind can absorb. Can it continue? You bet it can! We are about to be introduced to two of the finest people we had met on this trip! Eliane and Alain Yoncourt are the epitome of French charm and from the beginning wanted only to see that we had a wonderful experience to the Cote d'Amor, and Eliane was fluent in English. Halleluia! At last Maggie can be free of me for a while! We were shown to our lovely bedroom on the 4th floor, overlooking the valley, and chosen (I am sure) for us since we are artists and need to see the countryside without anything interfering with the view! The room was beautifully decorated and protected by the resident spirit of Pol- de- Leon who Madame had seen, and unfortunately, we did not during our visit.

We had arrived later than expected and missed dinner, but Madame said, "Do not worry! I will make a light supper for you." The light supper turned out to be an aperitif, soup, salad, cheese and dessert, all served by the roaring fire in the fireplace! Our days and nights of starvation seemed very far in the past.

The next morning, we were greeted by a typical French breakfast of freshly baked croissants, confiture, beure, hot tea or coffee! We ate like starving artists should, wondering if our days of starvation would be the same there. We were taking no chances! We would be on our own during the day. During breakfast, we chose the meat or seafood we would have for dinner that evening. And dining in the beautiful dining room was a highlight!

Outside our room was a display of antique Christening gowns, wedding dresses, and other relics worn by past occupants of the Chateau. I wondered how their life was here, and if their spirits remain and would give me insights into their lives of living, loving and playing. I wondered how the experiences Maggie and I are having in France will affect us when we go back home.

Sunflowers by Viles.

For some reason, I was having a hard time painting on this trip. Was I so wrapped up in the French people, their lives, and their language that I was losing my perspective? With only three more weeks to go, would I be able to overcome this problem? Usually, when I travel to paint I just opened my backpack. Take out my paints, put a large piece of watercolor paper on my easel and go. This trip it is not so easy. I prayed that I was not making things hard for myself by being so wrapped up in the people and places. I supposed time would tell. The real answer would come when I get home and see what I do with all the information I have gathered during the weeks we traveled.

One afternoon, Maggie decided to paint from the window in the foyer outside our room. She opened the shutters, sat on the floor, set out her sketchbook, and proceeded to paint the beautiful landscape. Suddenly, a pigeon flew into the room, circling around her, flapping his wings, making a lot of noise and coming dangerously close to the antique garments on the bed!

"Oh gee!" she said. She heard Madame coming up the stairs conducting new guests on a tour of the Chateau. They were greeted by Maggie jumping up and down, waving her arms, and shouting "Go away! Go 'way!" to a bird that had just flown out the window. As Madame and the visitors descended the stairs we heard her say, "Maggie is a talented artist if a bit eccentric!"

One of our excursions from the Chateau was to Perros – Guirec on the Isle de Brehat where we encountered huge reddish-pink rocks named menhirs. We ran around like idiots, climbing, sliding down the huge rocks, having fun on rocks that were as smooth as silk. The most interesting site was a house built between two massive menhirs that looked like mountains. They were so large. There was nothing else around and it seemed that the very high tides in that area would flood the place. Maggie described the area as "mammoth rocks hurriedly thrown around by giants interrupted in their task of building a second Stonehenge, this time on the French shore." It was a very good description of a mind-blowing place. Nearby was a megalithic tomb said to be the tomb of King Arthur.

Another interesting thing about this island was from where the ferry to Isle de Brehat leaves and to where it returns. It depended on the tides that are HUGE. At high tide, the ferry dropped us off at the port, and we could walk just a few feet to the village. But, at low tide, we disembarked about a quarter of a mile off shore and walked in on a long footbridge, which was covered at high tide. Very interesting! With all the walking we were naturally starving so we consumed a large seafood pizza for lunch prepared with seafood caught locally. Every minute of our day on the Island was fascinating, and this turned out to be one of my favorite places of the entire trip. It really resonated with me, and I knew I would return! I did two more times with my artist friend, Jim Scott, and his workshop participants. We had a wonderful time!

On returning to the chateau, we were exhausted and ready for dinner and bed. The next morning we were fine and set out to explore more areas around the Chateau. Every minute of our stay in this area gave us something interesting to paint. One day, when I was off painting somewhere, Maggie decided to explore. She found a magnificent display of white Clematis draping over a stonewall and fancy iron gate. This was just her cup of tea! Hoping it would be okay for her to paint there, she set up her stool and easel and began painting. Suddenly the gate opened and out walked tiny little Anna, the silver haired lady of the manor, walking with a cane and jabbering French a mile a minute! She was wearing pedal pushers! We had not seen those in the states in years! Maggie sputtered her few French phrases: "Je suis artiste qui peindre en France et nous irons to les Jardins de Monet a Giverny!" Anna welcomed her even though they could not converse. Anna invited us for lunch the next day and we met her husband and grandchildren.

Anna's house was typically French with a huge kitchen with gleaming copper pans hanging on the walls and the inevitable flowers that every French home displays. My copper pans at home are never polished! I don't use them since they are antiques. We toasted each other and our respective countries, and once again, Maggie and I were given a gift of France, one of many for me and another one for her.

Back at the Chateau, we were captivated by an enormous arrangement of flowers in a huge

Your author Pat painting in Monet's Garden.

crystal vase sitting on the lace covered foyer table and in front of a gold framed mirror. There was also a large golden candelabra that was breathtaking and Maggie had to paint it. Permission granted, she began working and I just made a sketch, hoping I would paint it after returning home and eventually I did.

Maggie had never been interested in painting flowers in vases. She loved cascading vines and flowers over walls, fences, and gates, clumps by the roadside, birds in marshes, seashells by the seashore; really anything pertaining to nature. Where her work is inspired by nature and is impressionistic with soft colors, mine leans more toward abstract, non-objective, expressionistic,

Maggie and Pat at Chateau.

lots of color, huge canvases, large pieces of silk stretched on wooden stretchers, and collage. After the silk is stretched, I use resist to draw the lines that hold in the color, and then paint with French dyes. These paintings are very expressionistic. I love the diversity and will try anything to get the effect I strive for. I have never been an artist who likes to draw or was even good at drawing, so going to Giverny was going to be a real challenge for me, and one to which I was looking forward.

Eventually, it was time for us to go. Leaving the Chateau was sad but go we must for Giverny and Les Jardins de Monet were waiting! On the way we stopped at a small patisserie and bought barbecued chicken and loaf of unwrapped bread. Sitting beside a 1,000 year old church, we picnicked and sketched in a field carpeted with flowers. We were unnaturally quiet, thinking about our experiences so far, and contemplating what was in store for us in Giverny. Before going to Giverny, we had to be juried so we each sent an essay and some examples of our work along with the date we wanted to be there. Finally our excitement reached a state of frenzy. We were so close! Would something happen to keep us from the highlight of our trip?

We were scheduled to stay in rooms on the Anderson Farm, owned by Patricia and Ian Anderson, an English couple who had retired to Veteuil to raise horses. Their farm was about five miles from Giverny. We had two bedrooms with a kitchen between so we could do our own meals. The apartment was located above the horse stalls. What could be better? Monet painted in a barn!

During our weeks on the road, we had gone from gourmet to near starvation and were looking forward to being able to prepare our own meals. We began our version of "Garbage Soup" using the remains of the barbecued chicken and some vegetables and condiments we had on hand. That was one chicken that gave its all for a good cause! We knew we would have a kitchen to use so on the way from Brelidy we found a town with a market and bought vegetables, fruit and bread. It is a good thing we did because we were facing such a busy schedule food would have to be secondary. Every day we would add more water and veggies to the pot. At the end of the two weeks, I doubt there was any food value! Thank goodness there were patisseries where we could buy sandwiches, quiches, croissants, etc. so we survived.

Sleeping, however, was a different story. During our first night Maggie's horse was active all night, neighing, stomping his feet and generally making a fuss. Maggie thought I was in the bathroom, sick, and called out, "Pat – Pat—are you okay?" On arising the next morning I looked at Maggie and said "Maggie! You look awful!" She groaned and said, "My horse kicked all night!" This continued the entire time we were there. Some nights it was my horse making such a racket and others, Maggie's. There was nothing we could do about it but it sure did take some getting used to and we were exhausted!

Patricia and Ian were having trouble training the horses that came to them from Poland. I suppose they did not understand English and their training was not going good. They were running around, stomping their feet and trying to run away, perhaps back to Poland! The menagerie of animals on the farm included a huge sheep dog named Sultan, a beehive, and a 15 year old chicken named Hillary. They enjoyed having us around and were good company for us while we painted interesting subjects on the farm.

The English cutting gardens with the myriad of colors were gorgeous on the hill close to the farm. Since the gardens were open to the public Tuesday through Sunday we could not be there from 10:00 am until 5:00 pm. So we came back home to paint or would go to other places nearby like Vernon or Valence. We were only five miles from the farm to Giverny but it took about 20 minutes for the drive on a narrow country lane. During that ride we passed by a small village off to the right, Cherence, and we renamed it Brigadoon. It was beautiful in the rain and mist and seemed to be floating along the crest of the hill on which it rested. The church steeple and the roofs of the houses were beautiful against the clouds and the yellow fields showing through the mist were like a vision. What a lovely gift to us every morning as we passed by! We often stopped to photograph and paint there. One Sunday we stopped to paint and suddenly were treated to a mini Tour de France with about 50 bicycles passing by just as the church bells began to ring.

Monet's Roses.

What can I say about Monet's Gardens? They were beautiful, planted in two sections, the Clos Normand and The Lily Pond is filled with flowers of every color and variety. It took 20 years for Monet to complete the Lily Pond! Monet said, "I am good for nothing but painting and gardening! My greatest masterpiece is my garden!" One can read about his gardens, see photos but to really appreciate his accomplishment, one must go there to experience the peace, tranquility and spirituality of the place.

Painting in the gardens was almost over-powering! To walk the path of the most revered painter in France had walked, see the gardens he had lovingly cultivated and made famous in his paintings, feel his spirit in the house in which he and his family lived, was almost more than we could take in. Fortunately, there were other lovely gardens in Giverny so we would paint there when we could not be in Monet's Gardens. This was the beginning of the Impressionists Trail and many of the gardens were also painted by other now well-known artists. There was no lack

Sunflowers near Giverny

of subjects for us to paint.

Giverny is a small village by the River Seine in Eastern Normandy. Monet first found the village in 1883, fell in love with the beauty of Giverny, and later returned and rented a farmhouse eventually buying it and two acres of land. Those two acres became what is now the renowned gardens. Winding paths lead around the small brook, Ru, that feeds the lily pond, with mature trees all around. Monet was infatuated with water lilies. Loving the beauty of the lilies, he painted them 250 times!

The Clos Normand was very different in that it was laid out in rectangular beds. The plants were allowed to flop around and nasturtiums were planted and let spread eventually covering even the paths. Monet planted flowers and herbs, lilacs and other plants with distinct perfumes to enhance the senses and other plants. These helped draw visitors more and more into his world.

I felt cheated since I have no sense of smell!

The winding path along the banks of the pond leads to the green Japanese bridge crossing the pond. Along the rails that make up the bridge are cascades of lilacs and wisteria in purple, pink, and white floating downward, mirroring the weeping willow trees with their lovely hanging branches dancing in the light wind. I wondered if the bridge and plantings were inspired by the Japanese print collection he had in his home. I later discovered that they were. When I was in Tokyo a few years later and saw the blooming cherry trees planted on the banks of small man-made channels of water that run through parts of the city I was immediately transported back to Giverny and Monet's Garden!

Below the bridge the lily pond flows gently causing the lily pads to move as if they were waltzing. The morning light gives a mysterious appearance to the reflections of flowers growing on the banks. One of the gardeners told me that they still use a flat bottom rowboat, an exact replica of the one Monet used, to clean out leaves and other debris. The pond is only about two feet deep.

I have to admit the lily pond was fascinating with its dark shadows, reflections of the sky, flowers and trees. Each lily was a painting in itself. There was an air about the gardens like they were waiting for the master to return. I did not do much painting but took lots of pictures and wrote in my journal. Usually, I am not a flower painter. It is interesting that 30 years later, as I was preparing for a museum exhibition, I went into my studio one morning to begin a new painting. This painting would be included in the museum show, and it turned out to be the first in a series of the gardens!

I had been working on a different watercolor technique where I sprayed the paint on Yupo, a very different type of paper that was, in fact, plastic that was mostly used for posters and signs. One morning I sprayed three large pieces of the Yupo with the watercolor and left them to dry. The next morning when I went back to my studio I was blown away. The first one was Monet's lily pond! With only a bit of tweaking the lilies were more evident. The other two paintings turned out to be sunflowers and other species of flowers from the gardens. Eventually there were nine flower paintings inspired by Monet's garden and now I have become a flower painter along with the other diverse techniques I like to do. Who knows what life and 30 years can bring?

Each morning we would leave the farm about 7:00 am to go into the garden at 8:00 am and paint until 10:00 am when the tour buses arrived and throngs of people descended on us. We packed up at 10:00 am and left to paint in other places, knowing we could come back at 5:00 pm and stay until dark. On Mondays we could go in early and stay all day until dark.

One favorite place to paint outside the garden was Vernon, just across the river, and we chose their market day to go there. Another of my favorites was Valence, a small village not far away. Markets are found in every village and there is one open somewhere every day including weekends. They are interesting places to get ideas for painting. They are busy, colorful, exciting, and had plenty of available food for us to take home! Color was everywhere and so were lots of people. Maggie did very beautiful paintings while there!

There were other gardens in Giverny where we could paint when we were not in Monet's gardens. Giverny was the beginning of the Impressionist Trail, and many artists came to paint in the other gardens in Giverny along with that of Monet. His list of artist friends reads like a who's who in the art world of that epoch: Renoir, Sisley, Bazille, Courbet, Boudin, and Jong were the ones he admired the most. Once again, everywhere we looked there was a subject crying out to us, "Paint me! Paint me"! The flowers around his house and studio were incredible, colorful, and the combinations of species interesting. I could visualize Monet painting at his easel in the beautiful morning light.

One Monday, a group of tourists were allowed in the gardens for 20 minutes even though the gardens were closed to the public that day. They were in such a hurry they walked on our paintings that were on the ground beside us. They never apologized and left footprints on some of them. Later we just painted the marks out! I learned from that experience to be more careful when there are lots of people around. I apparently had not learned that lesson during all the field trips I had made to paint on location, but then I was mostly alone. The last Monday we arrived at the garden to find television cameras throughout. A crew was preparing a documentary to be shown on an educational TV channel. I suppose we were included in the filming but never got to see the finished film. Artists are not usually dressed for TV when working outside so it is a good thing we did not see the final film! However, when we returned home I got a call from friends from London who had see the TV program and were not happy that we had not come to visit them since we were close! The next year I did go to London and spent some time with them!

On Mondays, local artists are allowed to paint in the gardens too. The first Monday we met Pierre Bittar, from Versailles, who said he came most Mondays. He was very complimentary of our work especially Maggie's. Maggie is a master at quick watercolor sketching while I am not and never will be. Pierre is considered the modern day Monet in France. His work is beautiful. Back at home I bought a magazine that featured his work.

One of the best paintings I did in the gardens was of a rooster I named Mr. Monet. He hung around me all day the first Monday, only leaving when the tour bus arrived and coming back when they left. He and I chatted all day, and he critiqued my work! He pecked around on my palette getting watercolor on his beak, and watched quietly while I painted his portrait. After finishing, I asked him what he thought about it. That bird actually came closer, cocked his head and gave a loud "caw"! I took that to mean he approved!

One of the gardeners told me a story about Monet. One day Monet was standing by the fence looking out over the gardens when a neighbor walked up and said,"Ah, Claude, I see you are playing today!" Monet replied,"No, today I am working!" The next day Monet was near the same spot with his easel and the beginning of a painting. The same neighbor came by and said, "Well, today I see you are working!" Monet's reply was. "No, today I am playing!" I can relate to that! When I am in my studio the hours fly by, and at the end of the day, I am tired but very happy to have spent the day playing with my paint and brushes. Work, for an artist, is not painting itself but preparation for the painting he or she will do, is.

After two weeks of living in Monet's world, we had to leave. The time to go home was drawing near and we had another adventure to look forward to. We went to a suburb of Paris to spend a couple of days with longstanding friends of mine, Anne and Claude Sacher. Once there, Anne took us into Paris to visit the Musee de l'Orangerie where the huge paintings Monet did of the lily pond during his last years are now located. These paintings were a gift to the French people by Monet's son, Michel, who was his heir. The room they were in was circular and the display was breathtaking. These paintings were not so detailed as were his usual work because in his later years he suffered with cataracts. They were more abstract and were obviously done with the love and spirit Monet put into all his work, and were considered to be the forerunner of abstraction.

Our drive to the home of my friends, the Sacher's, was easy and once again we were wined and dined, shown interesting places and enjoyed the French hospitality to which we had become accustomed. Claude and Anne had visited my family along with the Huet de Guervilles on two occasions. They are like family. Once we three couples met in New York City to see the sites and attended the play, "Cats." I got in trouble with people around us because of having to translate the story for them!

So, our journey had come to an end, and we went home, filled with memories to last a lifetime. We left with memories of places we had seen, portfolio and sketchbooks filled with work we had done, experiences we had, people we had met and plans to return. And return we did; several times, to different parts of France, revisiting some the places we had been before, and taking friends with us to share the country Maggie had come to love as much as I did. Later, she took several people for workshops she taught, and I made the decision to give up traveling so much and become a real artist, a decision I have never regretted.

Maggie and I have stayed in touch over the years. She still goes to France often and recently she visited me here in North Carolina and we enjoyed a few days of painting together and reminiscing about the adventures we had shared. As I write this Maggie and her husband, Peter, are in France and will then go to Germany to visit relatives. Life goes on!

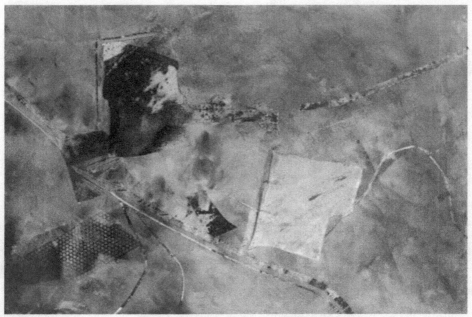

The Shallow Pond. French dye on Silk by Viles.

ASIA

What are the chances an obscure artist from North Carolina would be invited to participate in International exhibitions in China, Japan, and Korea? Not good I thought, but that happened to me thanks to a lovely Korean American lady, Kichung Lee Lizee. I met Kichung when she and my friend Vae Hamilton, taught a painting workshop at Cheap Joe's Art Store in Boone, North Carolina Vae was teaching watercolor and mixed media, and Kichung taught Oriental calligraphy and how it could be used in our paintings. It was fun experience, and I learned a lot about Oriental calligraphy and how to use it in my own work. I also learned that I would NEVER learn how to do the real Oriental calligraphy!

Kichung is a special and very spiritual lady. We became friends, and she introduced me to Ed and Polly Gast, who on the second Sunday afternoon each month had a gathering in their home in the mountains. These meeting were very spiritual and meant a lot to all of us who attended. There were always several people there each Sunday and we all became good friends and continued these meeting for about two years. Unfortunately, life intervened and after two years I had to stop attending. But Kichung and I kept in touch and one day Kichung called and asked me if I would consider participating in an art exhibit in China, and said our friend Vae Hamilton was invited too. Never in my wildest dreams did I think I would ever be invited to exhibit my work in an International art exhibit in Asia. I agreed and was then introduced by telephone to Kim Juhwe who lives in Seoul, Korea with his wife, Hanako. From here on I will refer to Kim using the ending "san." Both Kichung and Kimosan are Korean. Kimosan asked me to send my paintings to him and he would be responsible for taking them to China. I was to meet Kichung and Kimosan in China. Such excitement. I could hardly control myself just thinking about what a wonderful experience this would be. Unfortunately, Vae was unable to make the trip with me.

My family thought I was crazy for even thinking about undertaking such a journey. I paid no attention to the fear mongers. Tone Duncan, a friend who was born in Japan and now lives in North Carolina, gave me the name of an excellent travel agency that specialized in Asian travels. The agency is located in Atlanta, Georgia, and if I remember correctly, the name of the agency is IACE Travel. I contacted the agency to schedule my flights and make hotel arrangements. The gentleman I worked with was interesting to talk with, and knew exactly what I needed. Plans were made weeks in advance, airline tickets bought, paintings sent to Kimosan and arrangements were made for my two "fur babies," Red Dog and Spencer to stay in an exceptional kennel near the Charlotte, North Carolina airport. The agency had also arranged for me a side trip to Xi'an to see the recently discovered tomb of the ancient Chinese Emperor Qin Shi Huang who reigned in the Third Century BCE. His tomb had been discovered in 1974 by local farmers in the Lintong district of Xi'an. An excavation of this ancient tomb was undertaken, and about 8,000 Terracotta soldiers, 150 chariots, and 520 horses, all sculpted out of clay and full size were discovered. However, the majority of these remain buried in the main pit near Quin Shi Huang's Mausoleum. Other non-military figures in other pits of the same grave include officials, acrobats, strongmen and musicians. Xi'an is also the beginning of the famous Silk Road. The day I was to leave for Beijing I woke up at dawn and being so excited, I could not go back to sleep. I got up and began final preparations for the journey. Thank goodness I had arranged for my two dogs, Red Dog and Spencer (brothers), to stay in an exceptional kennel close to the Charlotte airport from where I would begin my flight. Their necessary things: medications, special food for Red, and their toys

Preparing for a festival in Kyoto.

had to be packed, and last-minute things had to be put in my suitcase. After a shampoo and set for my hair, I was flying around the house like a madwoman, praying I would not forget something important. My sketching materials, watercolor paints, brushes, and camera were waiting by the door. I heard a loud boom; a crack of thunder and lightning and a torrential rain began falling. It had been raining all night, but I did not know that a real thunderstorm was imminent. The rain was incredible. I could barely see out the window. I said to myself, "Self, this WILL stop. It must." IT DID NOT. I drove very slowly all the way to Charlotte, dropped the boys off at the kennel in a downpour, then drove to the airport, parked and went into the terminal. By then I was soaking wet.

Fate intervened. My flight was delayed because of the storm. My connecting flight in Chicago was also delayed since they were having storms too. After fourteen hours and 30 minutes sitting on Concourse A, the Charlotte airport closed. I was exhausted from the long wait and had read both books I had brought for the two long flights. I had been given a new flight time to go out early the next morning. I left the airport in a downpour and a little voice in my head told me to pick up Red Dog and Spencer from the kennel and GO HOME. They were happy to see me, and it turned out to be an excellent move. The drive home was harrowing with the torrential rain falling, thunder and lightning and the dogs were very nervous. It was a long drive.

The fast train to Kyoto.

The next morning, I got up at 3:00 am to prepare to leave at 5:00 am. I loaded the boys and luggage and started down the driveway. The fog was so thick I could not see the driveway curve. I slowly turned around, went back to the house in time to pick up the ringing phone. It was the airport calling to tell me it was closed, and there would be no more flights for me that day. What to do? It was Wednesday, the flight to China would take nearly 24 hours and the opening reception of the exhibit was early Thursday evening and there was no way I could get there in time.

I didn't know how to get in touch with Kichung and Kimosan to let them know what happened. We were staying in the same hotel in Beijing, but I didn't know its name so there was no way to contact them to let them know what was going on. They were to meet me at the airport. I was concerned that they would go to the airport and not know why I was not there. Fortunately, they did learn about the airport in Charlotte being closed because of weather and assumed I would not arrive. I placed a call to the travel agency who graciously cancelled my flights. They told me there would be a voucher from the airline I could use for other flights. My paintings for the exhibit had been shipped ahead so they were in the exhibit, thanks to Kimosan.

I was so disappointed. I notified the travel agency of the problem and they in turn contacted the Chinese agency that had made the arrangements for my tour to the ancient grave site of Qin Shi Huang. I was told that the fee for the tour was not refundable. I lost $4,000 on that deal. The airline, however, did give me a voucher that I used later for two domestic flights.

The next year, 2006, Kimosan invited my friend Vae Hamilton and me to bring our paintings

Kyoto.

to Japan and participate in an exhibit in Tokyo planned by him and Kichung. I accepted but unfortunately Vae could not go. I began preparing for the trip, and made arrangements for my dogs, Spencer and Red, to stay in the same kennel I had planned on them staying in for the China trip.

This was the beginning of my association with the Chinese, Japanese, and Korean artists. I now have eight volumes of exhibition catalogs from those countries with my work in them from the various exhibitions I have shown in. And, yes, they are mostly printed in traditional Oriental writing and I can't read them, but the photos of my paintings are excellent. Vae could not go nor did she send her paintings. It would have been much more fun if she had gone with me.

However, when my good friend, Tom Oakley, learned about me planning to go to Japan alone he said emphatically, "No. You are not. You might not be safe traveling alone. I won't hear of it. I have always wanted to go to Japan so I am going with you." I was happy about that. Unfortunately, Tom's life partner, Tim, could not go with us and he would have been a lot of fun too.

Tom and I made our plans and on March 25, 2005, we drove to Charlotte and were lucky to find a motel near the airport that had two rooms available. I could hardly believe how much I missed Spencer and Red Dog in just one night away from them. When I dropped them off at the kennel, they were not happy. Spencer hung his head and would not look at me. Red Dog just stared at me, and I could tell he couldn't believe I was really leaving him. This trip may turn out to be a long two weeks.

Early the next morning, we boarded the plane in Charlotte and began our 6346 mile flight to Tokyo. Lift off. I couldn't believe I was actually traveling to Japan.

Karam Gate at Nuo Castle.

I could hardly believe how much I missed the dogs in just one night away. This might turn out to be a long two weeks.

On the flight we met some Americas who lived in Japan and they told us a lot about what to expect. They said it would be very cool there, lots of traffic, interesting people, lots of history and spectacular scenery. I would be learning some Japanese phrases like, "Hello, my name is Pat. Where's the ladies room? What time is it?"

Tom was a dream to travel with. This was the first time in all my travels that I had needed help with luggage, but this trip was different. I had a huge red suitcase full of paintings for the exhibition, a small suitcase for my clothes, a backpack for my painting supplies, and a purse.

The following is an excerpt from my journal:

The flight smooth so far: We just passed over Saskatoon. There's lots of snow. The land masses below are delineated by roads that resemble metal fences from so high above the ground. There are spots of turbulence. 9 hours 28 minutes until arrival. Can't go to sleep. Guess it is time to take the sleeping pill the doctor gave me. Tom called me at 4:00 am this morning and I slept very little during the night. I was not prepared to miss the boys so much. Spencer was so sad when I left him and his brother Red at the kennel in Charlotte. He hung his head and refused to look me in the eyes. I feel guilty. They have not been away from me very much and they are young. 6 hours 32 minutes since we left Atlanta. We are over the Gulf of Alaska: 3563 miles to go. We are trying to sleep but it is not easy. Just crossed Cook's Inlet: four more hours to destination. We just crossed the Bering Sea and International Date Line: It is already tomorrow. During the flight so far, sleeping has been nearly impossible. The roar of the plane, people moving around, four seats on our side of the airplane, and Tom and I have the middle two. It is nearly impossible to get to the aisle to walk around a bit. However, the seats recline enough to feel almost flat. If the two passengers go to the lounge at the same time, it is possible to lie down on all four of the seats. They left and Tom said "Pat, if you go to the lounge I can lie down." My reply? "When Hell freezes over. You leave and I will take a nap." We had a good laugh and stayed the way we were.

We finally arrived in Tokyo and were met at the airport by Kimosan and Kichung. It was wonderful seeing her again and finally getting to know Kimosan, the gentleman with whom I had exchanged so many phone calls. His English was better than my Japanese could ever be. I learned a few words on the airplane and had forgotten them. They took us to the beautiful Imperial Hotel in the center of Tokyo. It was huge and nothing like what I had expected. Having never been to Tokyo, I knew nothing about the city, its size, how modern it was, and how friendly everyone was. Tom and I were both blown away. After dinner, we went to our rooms and had a good night's sleep.

After breakfast the next morning we learned that Kichung and Kimosan had a full day planned for us. They came to the hotel to get us. First, we went to the Art Center, within walking distance of the hotel, to see the exhibit gallery and become acquainted with the staff and volunteers who were in charge. The center is modern, spacious, and the paintings well hung. I was impressed. It was a beautiful venue to hold and art exhibit.

After that visit, we went on a tour to see the famous Hot Springs where we learned if we ate an egg that had been boiled in the Springs, we would live seven years longer. I didn't try one. After that we were taken to visit a silk factory that produced the most beautiful silk kimonos I had ever seen. They were made from silk hand-painted by local artists. It was fascinating to watch the artists painting, and I learned a trick or two that became useful in painting my own large expressionistic paintings on silk. I use a special dye for the paintings, but the paintings are not as spectacular as those kimonos. The detail in the designs was mindboggling.

After that visit, we were taken by car to other interesting areas of the city. The city itself is clean and beautiful. Everything looked new. I loved the man-made channels filled with water that flowed throughout. The blooming cherry trees planted on the banks dropped their pink petals in the water and that reminded me of the water lily pond in Monet's Garden in Giverny, France where I had painted for two weeks in 1993. After that tour we went back to the hotel to rest. I must say that our rooms there were wonderful.

Kimosan and his wife, Hanako, who speaks some English, came for us early for dinner and then escorted us to the Art Center for the reception and opening of the exhibit.

Tom and I were the only Americans in attendance that evening. Kichung did an excellent job of translating for us and Tom and I both had a wonderful time. After the reception we were escorted back to the hotel. Then Kichung gave us an itinerary of what they had planned for us. Fortunately, Hanako was able to go with us often and that made conversation easier for Tom and me.

I had done quite a bit of research on Tokyo, and there were a few places I wanted to visit. One was Mount Fuji. It can be seen from nearly every part of the city. It is 12,000 feet high. The peak was always covered with snow and on the crest of the mountain is a Shinto Shrine. Shintoism is the native religion. Buddhism was introduced to Japan in the Fourth Century BCE by China and Korea. Both Shintoism and Buddhism are practiced by nearly all the Japanese people. The city was fascinating and everyone we came in contact with were very helpful and made sure we had a good time and saw as much as possible. Knowing we would have to come back to Tokyo to take our flight home, we asked if it would be possible to go to Kyoto. Kimosan said yes and we made plans to go the next day. He took us to the train station, helped us buy our tickets, and escorted us to the gate. We thought we were going on a tour. Nope. We were on our own.

Surprise. The American couple we had met at the airport were there, and they helped us put our tickets into the ticket machine. Suddenly the tickets flew out of the machine, bells began ringing, the gate slammed shut on my knee, and we were surrounded by authorities. Tom and I were ready to run when someone told us we had been overcharged for our tickets by $40 and we had to wait for a refund and new tickets. That took a few minutes, but we still made the train. We did not know until we were on the train, and it was flying over the tracks, that we had to change trains on this trip. Thank goodness our new friends helped us navigate through that experience.

Even though it was a fast train we would not arrive in Kyoto until late. And we were starving, not having had time to eat. We assumed there would be a chance to buy food on the train. No food. No water.

However, the train ride itself was great. Flying along those tracks was interesting. There were huge beds of tea plants alongside the tracks growing in perfect rows up the hillsides, not a weed in sight, not a ripple on either side of the rows. They were a sight to behold, manicured unlike any garden I had ever seen. I was impressed. No garden around my home looked like those did.

Further along we saw rice paddies that were just as beautifully laid out, well maintained and as interesting as the tea rows. They were still dry, waiting for their growing season to begin. They would then be flooded with water to begin their growth. What a beginning to a wonderful couple of days in the beautiful city of Kyoto. My Japanese friend from home, Tone Duncan, who is a native of Kyoto, had told me a lot about the city and we were not disappointed.

Kyoto became capital in 754, surrounded on three sides by mountains which makes it easier to protect. Two rivers run throughout the city.

Niga Castle is covered with 20 kilograms of gold leaf. The gardens were gorgeous. The pine trees were sculpted into amazing and beautiful shapes. The original castle was destroyed by fire and rebuilt in 1954. It was very cold and misting rain the day we were there.

We saw Buddhist Temples with statues of Buddhas. Bright red Shinto shrines were everywhere. These shrines were actually very small houses, built on stilts and painted a beautiful true red color. Around the mountain there are 100 small Shinto shrines for lesser spirits to live in when they come to visit. I really wanted to have three or more built in my woods but never could find anyone who would build them from just a drawing I made. Each time you go through a Tori (gate) you are purified. I could feel the spirits even though there were a lot of people around the area. It was very cold and windy. Everything we saw and did was interesting.

The next morning, Tom and I walked a long time in Kyoto center after a light breakfast of scones and coffee. We accidently discovered a Shin Buddhist Temple with a service in progress. The priests were chanting, playing gongs, etc. We sat on a bench. God was there. The place was filled with Spirit. I wish I could have understood the chanting. I felt more in tune with the Japanese people and much respect for them and their nation. Our two days there passed much too quickly and neither Tom nor I wanted to leave. But a schedule had to be followed and the next morning, we boarded the Shinkansen – Bullet train, supposedly the "Super Express" that stoppedat every town. Three hours back to Tokyo. THIS TRAIN FLEW.

Our friends met us at the train station in Tokyo, escorted us back to the hotel and then took us to lunch. This is a good time to say that the food we had in Japan was outstanding. For me, the best thing was Sushi. I must say that if you ever eat Sushi in Japan, you will never eat it in the states again. It was spectacular. So fresh. The night before we left for home, we were taken to a special restaurant and all the nice people we had met during our visit came with us: sort of a going away party. The waiters kept bringing out individual small trays, one after another, of delicious food. Each tray was decorated with a small plant or fresh flower. Each tray was different than the one before, and they were beautiful. Tom was a bit reticent when he saw the food which was mostly raw, but he was a good sport and ate everything except the last one and I must be truthful. I had to close my eyes to eat that one and I swallowed it whole. Making eye contact with our food was a bit daunting but we managed. It was a riotous evening with all the new friends we had made joining us. What a way to end a wonderful trip.

Tom and I had a wonderful visit in Japan. How could we not? We were treated like family, taken to beautiful and interesting places, ate delicious food so different from what we have at home, participated in a wonderful art exhibition, and had enough memories to sustain us for a long time.

It didn't seem possible that this trip was nearly over. The two weeks had flown by. I didn't realize when I left home how badly I needed to get away for a while and what a way to do it. I was thinking much more clearly on this trip, and looking forward to being at home again with my boys, Spencer and Red Dog. This trip had given me a lot to think about, and a new perspective on a different part of the world. I am finding it difficult to put into words all that had happened, all the experiences I have had, and the different feelings I have been dealing with the last few months. The Japanese people were wonderful, happy, very giving, and were constantly doing things to make our visit special. My suitcase was full of small meaningful things they gave me but none of those things meant as much as the warm feeling of love, acceptance, and friendship they showered on Tom and me, and I am sure Tom felt the same way. I hope someday to see them all again.

Tom was a rock. I don't think I could have made this trip work if he had not been with me. We had a wonderful time together, laughing, talking, walking, learning new things, etc., I could not have had a better traveling companion.

Since that trip, my Japanese friends have kept me supplied with their wonderful teas. And after I returned home, I wrote a poem and sent a copy to my friend, Tone, who in turn sent it to the travel agency in Atlanta, who then sent it to the Imperial Hotel in Tokyo. Tone told me later the hotel had it framed and it is now in the lobby of the hotel. Maybe someday I will get to see it there.

Asian Odyssey

I returned last night from a land far away
Where cherry tree blossoms filled the sky
With a profusion of color
Reflected in the canals that run through the city
Like serpents.

A land surrounded by blue water and filled with
small people with open arms and big hearts.
A land of fast trains, rice paddies as dry as the desert
Waiting for the floods of spring to make them green.

Delicacies served on trays, each a picture of perfection.
A land of green tea, grown in manicured rows,
In tiny plots beside the train tracks,
And high in the mountains, tended by loving hands.

A land where giant Buddhas sit in temples
Where they have lived for 200 years.
A land of vermillion shrines, homes of the Shinto Spirits
That roam the world shedding light and love.

A land of Gardens of green
And water rippling in shallow ponds
With colorful Koi swimming and begging for food.
Color. A land of color.

Shop windows filled with clothes in colors of Spring
And beautiful Kimonos of hand painted silk
Shimmering in the morning light.
A land of mountains reaching for the sky,
Embracing the Gods, encircled by passing clouds,
With one mountain so high it is always covered
With a mantle of snow.

A land of huge cities filled with people.
A land that captured my heart
And I can't wait to return to---JAPAN.

I AM THE LUCKIEST WOMAN IN THE WORLD.

The next morning, we packed our luggage, had a light breakfast and were taken to the airport by Kichung and Kimosan. Saying goodbye was not easy. There were tears shed and promises made to stay in touch and perhaps be together again either in the states or Japan. How was I to

The Shallow Pond. French dye on silk by Viles.

know that it would only be a year before I would be back in Asia. Where? Korea.

Another adventure begins. An invitation (short notice) from Kimosan, a mad dash to get ready, another long plane ride, and a bus ride brought me into the city of Seoul, Korea and I will never forget the eight days I spent there. Kimosan invited me to sit on a panel of a symposium discussing art in the 21st century. I would be discussing art and answering questions on previously selected subjects. The subjects I would be discussing were: "What direction is art in the West taking in the 21st Century?", and "What influence has Eastern art had on Western art since World War II?" Being a representative of the West was a big job and one I did not feel qualified to do. Kichung would go with me as my interpreter. The desire to learn more about another Asian country and its customs won and I accepted. Before going to Seoul, I went to the North Carolina Museum of Art in Raleigh, our capital, and had a discussion with the historian about those two subjects. I learned a lot from him.

My first glimpse of Seoul was from the air, and it was beautiful. Long strings of lights on the many bridges glowed brightly and moved the traffic through the city. From the bus, I could see beautiful Christmas decorations, and it was obvious it would be even more beautiful in a few more days when the decorations were complete. Seeing all those Christmas decorations was a bit of a shock. I had no idea the Koreans practiced Christmas like we do in the States. I was impressed by my first view of the city of Seoul. The architecture was diverse and modern. The city had been rebuilt after the war between North and South Korea. The tall, tall buildings reached for the sky, and islands of isolated small spaces of old architecture in the old part of the city fea-

Pat, Tom, Hanako, and others at dinner.

tured small oriental style structures that were lovely.

My friend, Kichung, had flown with me. We took a bus from the airport to the bus stop near our hotel. A midnight trek, pulling our luggage, brought us near our hotel, the Sun Bee, but we were not sure which direction to turn. We were told it was located at the end of an alley in the oldest part of the city. The few streetlights were tiny and did not give off much light. We came to an intersection and discussed which way to turn to find the hotel. After a few minutes discussion I said, "I think it might be this way."

Kichung said, "How do you know? Have you been here before?"

I replied, "No. It just feels right." And it was. The little dark street led us to an old building in which the small hotel was located. We checked in and found our rooms to be nice, if small. Mine was well appointed and quiet. There was a hot and cold water set up for making coffee, tea, hot chocolate, and in the bathroom, there was shampoo, toothbrush, toothpaste, perfume. Everything we would need. And once again we were not asked for money or credit card or identification.

The difference in the time between home and Korea, fourteen hours, had created havoc with our inner clock, so sleeping was difficult. Awakening early, we had a typical Korean breakfast that was delicious. Little did I know that from then on, every meal would be almost the same and we would not have a regular table and chair. During the next eight days I think I walked a hundred miles, climbed 200 steps daily, and had all my meals sitting on the floor on thin cushions at a low table. The heated floor was wonderful. It melted the icicles off my butt. Being December, it was COLD. Very COLD.

At one event Kichung and I were taken to, we met a man who was a national treasure in Korea. He made traditional musical instruments by hand, also making the components he uses. He played one for me and it was beautiful. I really enjoyed hearing that. All the instruments he made were beautiful to see and listen to.

Kimosan introduced me to a lady who travel extensively throughout Korea lecturing on tea and teaching the traditional tea ceremony, sort of like the English High Tea. In America, if we have an afternoon tea with a friend, it is just a cup, maybe a cookie, and conversation. The tea lady is also an artist who designs and makes traditional Kimonas using hand-loomed and hand-painted silk. They were exquisite and expensive.

Memorial in Tokyo,

My new friends took me to musical performances of traditional Korean music that was different, and I enjoyed that very much. They also took me to a gorgeous shopping center, where the Christmas decorations were the most beautiful and elaborate I had ever seen. There were three floors of gorgeous fur coats in every style and color imaginable. Never had I been in a bookstore that covered a city block. It was a fascinating mall and very different from the shopping malls in the USA. It was also interesting to see so many Christmas decorations that were obviously Christian. There must have been some influential missionaries in Korea in the past. I was not expecting such shopping opportunities in Korea. Too bad I didn't have extra money for shopping!

The art exhibit I had traveled so far to attend and exhibit in was mounted in the Mulpa Art Center, an excellent modern venue. The artists' works were well hung with the paintings not placed too close together. We had been given a theme "Hands Across the Sea." I chose to interpret the theme using a spiral with figures meeting at the beginning of the spiral, their hands extended in greeting. The spiral was my own interpretation of an ancient Petroglyph I had seen on the side of a cliff in one of the canyons of the American Southwest. It was limited in size but

Exhibit with Asian Friends - Hickory Museum of Art

was the largest I had ever sent to Japan.

Our Native Americans believe that to copy an ancient petroglyph done by a Native American is a sacrilege, since they are, in most cases, religious. Others describe their daily activities, like hunting. My painting was done on canvas, made into a simple scroll and it did not need a frame. When it came back home, Kimosan had made it into a traditional Oriental scroll. It is beautiful and hangs in my home. I did not want to sell it. I am so lucky to have so many interesting, and wonderful people as friends from so far away.

As I wrote before, I was invited to sit on a panel of a symposium discussing art in the 21st Century. I would be discussing art and answering questions on previously selected subjects. The subjects Kimosan asked me to discuss were: "What Direction is Art in the West Taking in the

21st Century?" and "What Influence Has Eastern Art Had on the Western Art Since World War II?" Being the only representative of the West, was a big job, and I was not sure I was qualified to do it. Kichung was my interpreter. However, my desire to learn about another culture won, so I accepted.

During the symposium, I talked about how I thought Eastern art had influenced Western art and got into a discussion with one of the Chinese artists. My view about that issue was that Eastern art and calligraphy had certainly influenced Western art, especially since Eastern art tended toward minimalism. I also said that calligraphy was a beautiful way of writing and truly one had to be an artist to become proficient using it. I have tried calligraphy and failed miserably. He took issue with me and said he believed that calligraphy is mainly a method of communication even

Michiko Painting - Hickory Museum of Art

though it was used in their artistic endeavors. We argued back and forth for several minutes, then he bellowed to me and said, "Madame, I bow to your superior judgement.", in perfect English, everyone laughed, stood and bowed to both of us, then clapped their hands a long time. This was a highlight of the trip for me.

Another interesting thing I encountered in Seoul was the seating in restaurants. As I wrote before, the seating was on the floor on thin cushions, and it was awkward for me. One evening Kimosan took Kichung and me to a tearoom along with several of the artists participating in the symposium, and others I had met during my visit. Once again, we sat on the warm floor. I had a difficult time getting comfortable. My old bones were protesting. I am thankful I wore slacks that evening and continued to wear slacks during the remainder of the trip. We were served a large bowl of tea and platters of finger food. Several times the waiter came and refilled our bowls and added more tidbits to the food platter. There was entertainment and we sang along with the entertainers. I was singing in English, but to tell the truth, I was just mouthing the words because I can't sing. It was a wonderful fun filled evening and one I will always remember.

After we returned home, Kichung asked me if I could arrange an exhibition in our local museum for the Japanese and Korean artists as well as myself and my friend, Vae Hamilton, who had been invited to show her work in both Korea and Japan but could not go. I immediately went to the museum and talked with the director, Mickey Coe. Mickey was excited about the possibility, and we immediately began making plans. I called Kimosan and gave him the possible dates for the exhibit and he said he would let me know the details, the number of artists who would participate and when they would arrive. Later he called and told me the date and time they would arrive, how many were coming and they would bring their work with them.

This turned out to be a wonderful experience for all of us. There were eight visitors and they stayed with me in my home. We had makeshift beds everywhere. They spoke very little English. I spoke no Japanese or Korean, so Kichung and Kimosan were constantly busy translating for everyone. I participated in the exhibition with the paintings I had done while I was in the two countries, and Vae Hamilton also participated even though she had not been able to go with me on the two trips I made. It was a wonderful evening and will be long remembered by those of us who were there.

After the opening of the exhibition, I loaded everyone into my big van and took them on a trip to our beautiful mountains and then to several places closer to home. The group did not stay very long, just a few days.

On the night of the reception, we all went to dinner and they enjoyed a typical Southern meal. On arriving at the museum, they were happy to see lots of people and having Kichung and Kimosan there to help with the language problem made it more fun for everyone, especially the children. At one point Michiko, one of the artists from Japan, produced a very large piece of white paper she had put together with glue, spread it out on the floor, and announced she would do a demonstration of Japanese calligraphy. She also had mixed up a five gallon can of black ink using warm water and black ink powder. She told us after she finished her demonstration, we could all try to do calligraphy. There was much excitement.

Michiko, using a regular white floor mop as a brush, proceeded to demonstrate Oriental calligraphy. It was hilarious. While she was writing the calligraphy on the white paper, she would make a loud exclamation like---Hi-eee, stomping her feet occasionally. She was funny and everyone loved her. She invited all of us to participate, and we took turns. Even small children participated getting ink on their shoes and clothes. I wondered if their mothers ever got them clean.

We are lucky to have such a beautiful and delightful museum in our town. Now the museum collects and exhibits only the work of American artists. We recently had an major exhibition of work by the famous Andy Warhol. Many people attended the opening reception. For the three months the exhibit was on display, the museum was always full of people from several states and most counties of North Carolina.

About four years ago, I had a retrospective of my work covering 20 years of painting all over the USA, Asia and Europe. It was fun, well attended and my family was blown away. They didn't know I had been working so hard. That was my last exhibit in my hometown. Since then, I have had exhibitions in other states and a few in other countries. I needed a break.

MY BACKYARD NEIGHBORS

Living in the middle of a forest for the past 42 years has been a wonderful experience for me. I love the sounds of birds singing, talking with each other and the buzzing sound of the hummingbirds in flight is amazing. They move so fast it is like seeing a blur in the sky. And they, like many other birds, are territorial. One day, as I walked down the driveway, I saw a tiny little hummingbird nest hanging from a limb, the first I had ever seen. It looked like a miniature basket with long u-shaped handles. A hummingbird flew out of the nest and on closer inspection I saw two tiny eggs. I did not touch them. Every day, I looked at the nest and one day the eggs had hatched and the babies were unbelievably small, hardly recognizable as a bird. It is amazing how anything so small could live eve after they are fully grown.

One day, I walked by the kitchen sliding door and saw a dove just sitting quietly alone, or so I thought. She seemed to be staring into space, not moving a muscle. I watched her for a few seconds before I realized she was not alone. About two feet behind her another dove, a bit larger, was lying close by. Apparently, the bird had flown into the window and broke his neck. Every few minutes, I looked out and she was in the same position. After about an hour of sitting like that, not moving at all, she walked over, touched the dead one with her beak, then turned and flew away. On researching doves, I learned that they mate for life. I shed a few tears for the dead bird and his grieving mate that day and am thankful I have not seen that situation since. Yes, there have been many birds that have flown into the large windows throughout my house but so far, not another situation like the two doves. These deceased birds have their own graveyard, surrounded by large Quartzite rocks I have found in my woods and a large steppingstone that reads: REST IN PEACE.

There are many cardinals in our woods. I named them Sara and Bob to represent the numerous cardinals that fed at the feeding stations I have hanging in lots of places within sight of my kitchen windows. They are beautiful to watch particularly when the snow falls. They are very territorial and won't allow another of their breed close when they are feeding and heaven help if a bird of another species enters their space. In the winter their brilliant coloring is beautiful against the snow. Lately, I have noticed more cardinals than usual flying around, mostly the gorgeous red males.

Other beautiful birds I see regularly are woodpeckers. Mable and Gary represent a great number of their species including the large pileated woodpeckers. Recently, during a respite from torrential rain, I saw a male and female taking turns hunting insects around a tree trunk and taking the insects back to their nest. I did not know that the parents worked together in feeding their offspring. I like the rhythmic sound they make when pecking. It almost has a Morse Code like rhythm. Are they pecking to send messages, or searching for food on the tree limbs, or maybe sharpening their beaks? I don't know but sometimes the continuous pecking can drive you crazy if you are reading, watching TV, or just trying to chill out.

Just sitting at my kitchen table and looking out the wide expanse of windows is like watching a TV show! There is always something different to catch my eye. For instance, one day when I was having lunch, I looked up and saw a full-grown mountain lion walking down my driveway! I grabbed my camera and very quietly opened the door and snapped several pictures of him/her slowly walking toward the barn. It had been raining so I knew if he got off my driveway there would be footprints. I waited about an hour before I put my dogs on leashes and quietly walked down the driveway. I saw where the animal had gone back into the woods leaving footprints in the mud. After taking several more pictures of the footprints with mine next to them, we went back to the house, and I called the Science Center and told the person I talked with what happened. He informed me that we didn't have mountain lions in North Carolina and I said, "Well, we do now!" After I got pictures developed, I took them to the Science Center and the person I had spoken with was blown away! I never saw the animal again! Fortunately, some of my neighbors had seen him too, so there was plenty of proof that I was not imagining the creature. He/she was beautiful.

In 2015, I was invited to have an exhibition of my work at the Hickory Museum of Art. It was to be a retrospective of the past 20 years of my work as an artist and would open on September 6, 2016. In preparing for this exhibit, I thought of my backyard neighbors and decided to include them in the exhibition. Using a new technique I had been working on, I went to work and had a wonderful time painting the wonderful creatures I see daily. After several weeks of paying more attention to the creatures, began to see the different characteristics each one had. It was amazing!

Henry the raccoon came sneaking into the swimming pool area one day and ate all of the food I had put out for the feral cats. Two days later he was back with his wife and then a few days later they were back with their three children! This was the beginning of a situation I didn't know how to handle! If I stopped feeding the cats, would it hurt the pregnant one? Would they be able to manage? My plans were to try to trap them, one at a time and have them spayed. In order to do that I had to put out food. So, my plan if action went something like this: The cats usually came early in the morning, so I put out food for them then brought the bowls back in the house after they finished. Later in the day I fed them again, early afternoon, and that worked for a while. But the raccoons got wise! They never came in the morning, but they began coming early afternoon!

What to do? It was a dilemma, but I felt like I should feed the cats and I did enjoy them. They were tame enough to let me pet them. Finally, I had a solution to the problem.

Since the cats eat earlier than the raccoons, I put more food in their bowls so they could eat before the raccoons arrived. They left just enough for the raccoons to have a little! The cat's main meal would be in the morning and for the later feeding there would be a very small amount in the bowls for the raccoons! It worked! They came, ate the small amount, then left. They don't damage anything or, fight over the bowls. And I never found their poo or urine anywhere on the patios or walk! They have different characteristics too. Snoopy was a very pregnant lady who came to the bowl, looked around, and plopped on her tummy and ate two bowls of food! She was tense, always looked around to see if another raccoon is about to invade her territory. She finished eating, got a drink, and lumbered off into the woods.

After a while the raccoons got smart and began coming when the cats did! I had to put out a little more food and the different species ate together with no problems.

There was another raccoon family that came together. They seemed to talk with each other while eating and I would have loved to know what they said. Before evening is over all the bowls are empty and so was the gallon size water bucket. The water in the bucket became very dirty towards the end of the afternoon and it took a while for me to figure out that the raccoons were not only drinking the water, but they were also dipping their hands into it! Then I learned that raccoons do not have salivary glands, so they need a lot of water with their food. They dip their hands in the water then pick up the food. This is repeated several times during a feeding. They are very clean animals and I have seen them swimming in the swimming pool! So far there has never been a problem of fighting among them. While one eats, the others sit quietly by, waiting for their share. Another interesting thing about raccoons is that if the food runs out before they have had enough, they will come to the door and if they see me rub their hands together! I usually keep a bowl or two besides the door just in case!

Once, when I went out to feed, I began putting the bowls down. After they were all in place, I picked up a few things around the pool and came back to the door. The sliding door was slightly open. I must have failed to close it completely when I went out to feed the cats. It is a sliding door and if I push too hard it would bounce back. Nothing looked out of place in the bedroom. I went in, closed the door and walked down the hall to the kitchen. Sitting in front of the sliding door to the patio sat two young raccoons! They were watching the squirrels and chipmunks eating their food. Very quietly I eased around the island and got a handful of grapes out of the fridge. Raccoons love grapes! I squatted down behind them and said, "Hi boys! Want some grapes?" They turned toward me, reared on their back legs, rubbed their tiny little hands together, took one, and I began walking backwards to the bedroom, doling out one grape at a time. When we got to the bedroom sliding door, I opened it, backed out on to the patio, and they followed me!

Who says living in the woods is boring? I am careful not to get too familiar with these wild creatures and certainly don't want them to get their main food from me!

One evening just before dark a raccoon family, a mother, father and three youngsters showed up at the feeders. The youngsters ate a few bites then began nosing around the other bowls and among the flower beds. There was also the gallon bucket of drinking water for the animals. One of the three babies climbed on to the rim of the bucket and almost immediately, the other two climbed on to the rim too. Now, this was a small bucket that held about a gallon of water! They were trying to stay balanced to get a drink when one of the babies fell head first into the bucket! The mother continued eating! The two babies were making funny sounds and trying to stay balanced! The little one in the bucket did not have space to turn around and try to get out. I watched about 15 seconds, then, throwing caution to the wind, ran into the bathroom, grabbed a towel, ran out the door, pushed the two babies of the rim of the bucket, grabbed the one that have fallen, shook as much water off him as I could, then wrapped him in the towel to dry him off. It was autumn and rather cool! The little fellow was coughing and gasping for breath! Mom just kept eating! I put the fellow down, he shook himself and, finally, mom looked up, came to him and embraced him for a few minutes, turned toward me, nodded, then the entire family lumbered off. I sat down on the patio and had a good cry! I do believe she knew I meant no harm and was grateful I had saved her baby. Was there a chance the mom could have attacked me? Yep! But she didn't!

I am fascinated by the chipmunks! Rascal lives in the small garden outside of my bathroom. He was constantly making new underground routes for himself. But Rascal turned out to be a female who had five babies one early spring. It was fun to sit by bathroom window and watch their antics. They would suddenly dash under a leaf and disappear. I found several holes where they had dug tunnels and learned their tunnels can go as deep as ten feet. They can store three years of food in them! Do they have a special substance in their saliva that keeps the food from spoiling while it's is stored? I have no idea! I think they must hibernate since I don't see them for weeks during the cold weather and I don't know if they have more than one litter a year. They are so cute, faster than a blink of an eye and always uprooting the plants I put out in spring. I replant them and the next morning they are uprooted again! Sometimes they pull bulbs out of the ground and eat them. The ones who lived around the front porch are extremely messy. Every morning I look and find red clay dirt all over steps where they have excavated a new route! In fact, the entire yard is riddled with their tunnels along with other animals who make tunnels. After all these years I still have not figured out where they put the excavated dirt!

Sally, the turtle, has a story. Before the four lane Highway 321 was built the best way to drive to Charlotte was on Highway 16. One day when I was returning home from Charlotte,

I saw a movement in the middle of the road. It was large and beautiful turtle! It was as big as a dinner plate, bright yellow with black makings! I had never seen one like it before. Traffic was almost bumper to bumper, so I made a quick decision, stopped my car sideways in the middle of the road, stopping traffic in both directions, jumped out, picked it up and put it into my car. There was no way I would leave that beautiful turtle to be crushed by a truck or car! There were businesses on all sides of the highway and lots traffic, especially in late afternoon. There was no safe place for her to get to at the intersection and I knew she would never make it across the highway! Before arriving at home, I stopped at the supermarket to get groceries. When checking out I saw the *Our State Magazine* and on the cover was a picture of the turtle I had rescued! After putting the groceries away, I read the article, and learned she was a yellow-bellied slider, then considered to be an endangered species! I called the telephone number in the article and told the man I talked with what I had done. He was very happy I had saved a turtle! He told me what kind of turtle she was and how to take care of her. On my property there is very nice pond fed by a spring and where the spring comes out of the ground the water is no more than 8-10 inches deep. I was told to put her there and she would be fine.

I took her to the pond and turned her loose. That was several years ago, and I have seen her five times. Each time I would take her back to the pond! According to her size she was a female and now would probably be at least 30 years old and nearing the end of her life. I saw her about a year ago on my driveway and took her back to the pond! I thought she might be heading towards a very busy street where a lot of houses were built in subdivision behind my barn and pastures.

Hector the frog lives in the drain under the grilling station on my back patio! He and his offspring and/or friends have been there for years. When it rains and the drain is clogged, I use a long pole to clear it. Otherwise, the patio would flood and perhaps get into the kitchen and dining room. If Hector is inside the drain, he gets poked and is not happy about it! When I check the other side to see if the drain is unclogged, there he sits, scowling, and very indignant about losing his space! After all these years who knows how many frogs have been displaced from their favorite place? When a frog is not in residence, the chipmunks take the shortcut through the drain.

The deer families change every year when the new babies are born. Sometimes there is only one baby and other, twins. One year there were six fawns and five mothers! Then, one day there were six fawns and four mothers! What happened to the other mother? Something was wrong! Where was the other mother? Finally we learned she had been hit by a truck and killed so the herd adopted the fawn! I didn't get much work done then for watching the babies and their antics! They were fascinating to watch! After a few days I decided to begin feeding them. I have a lot of acreage around my home, most of which is the forest, and one of my neighbors does also.

Actually, they have three times the amount of acreage I have, but with all the houses built in the neighborhood, around us we didn't think there would be enough food for all of the deer to eat.

Other than our forest, there are not many wooded areas nearby for the deer to live and forage in. I went to the Tractor Supply Store, bought deer food and corn. Then I learned you can't feed corn to fawns because it makes them sick. So, during the birthing season they get only deer food. I don't give them much since they need to forage. Later I learned it was against the law to feed deer so I stopped. They still come around and eat grass but get no food from me.

An owl I named Barney, sits in a tree outside the great room nearly all day, every day. He would fly away occasionally, but he and his friends hooted all night in season. Once, there was a happening concerning Barney or another owl. One day I walked into the Great Room to search for a book on the coffee table. When I walked around to the side of the table nearest the fireplace, I heard a lot of loud flapping and screeching noise. I looked and saw a large bird sitting on the grate. It was dark in there and I could not tell what kind it was: just that it was large. I ran in to the kitchen, got a flashlight, shone it into the fireplace and was greeted by…a huge Barred Owl! I nearly had a heart attack! I couldn't figure out how he got into the chimney since there was a mesh covering over the opening. Finally, I realized the mesh covering the chimney must have rusted and when the bird landed on it, it gave in, and he fell at least 25 feet into the fireplace.

I sat down to think about what to do. I knew there was no way I could get the bird out alone, so I called the Wildlife Commission, told them what had happened. On doing so I was told they couldn't help me, that I should call an exterminator who would euthanize the bird and dispose of it! I said, "When Hell freezes over!" and hung up on them! Raptors are protected species and there was no way I would allow that to happen. I then called Animal Control and they told me the same thing!

After thinking a few minutes, I remembered that the two rangers at River Bend Park where I took my two dogs to play in the dog park, were bird experts, so I called and talked to Lori. She agreed to come help and asked if I knew someone who could help us. I said, "Yes!" and called Charlie Milfelt, a friend who also brought his dogs to the dog park, and he was happy to come. So, while I waited for them to arrive, I began wondering how long the bird must have been in the fireplace. I opened the door a crack, looked in and saw several places all over the floor, grate and logs where the bird had pooped and peed. I figured the bird had been captive in that space at least 24 to 36 hours, maybe longer, and would be hungry and thirsty. I went to the kitchen, got some fish, cut it into chunks, put some croutons and raisins in a bowl, got another bowl, and filled it with water. I slipped the food and water into the fireplace and went back to, opened the door and the food and water were all gone! I removed the dishes, then, leaving the door open a few inches, began talking to the bird. He sat very quietly while I told him help was on the way and we were going to get him out of his predicament. He would be safe and all he had to do was cooperate with us. He never moved a feather! He remained quiet but never took his eyes off me!

When Lori and Charlie came in, we sat for a few minutes talking about the best way to go about getting the owl out of his predicament. The fireplace is large, about five feet across, and there were two doors opening from the middle. We decided I would guard the left side of the doorway; Charlies would be in the middle to pry his talons off the grate; and Lori would get him out. I got two beach towels and brought them into the room. I opened the door completely, got into position and held a towel up on the left side so the bird could not get out. Charlie got into the middle, wearing gloves so he could pry the bird's feet off the grate, and Lori was on the right wearing heavy gloves, and had a beach towel in which she would wrap the bird. That wonderful bird never offered to harm us in any way! He never made a move to escape. He knew we were trying to help him. Lori was talking to him in a quiet voice the entire time.

Charlie got his talons loose and after several tries, Lori got the towel around the bird, pulled him out and he NEVER tried to fly, bite or make a dangerous move towards us. There is no doubt in our minds that he knew we were trying to help him, so he cooperated fully! I got a foam picnic cooler out of the closet and Lori put him into that. We went to the kitchen and talked about what to do. Lori suggested we call the Raptor Center in a nearby town, and she did. She and the veterinarian discussed the situation and best way to turn him loose. She asked Lori to use her smart phone to take the bird's picture and send it to her. Lori did and her quick response was, "The bird seems fine! I can't see any damage to his feathers, his eyes were clear, and his wings looked good. Take him outside and see if he could fly. If he flies, he is okay If not, try to catch him and bring him to us immediately!" Well, I though, whether that bird can fly or not, if we turned him loose, we will never again be able to lay hands on him!

Off to the backyard we went, put the cooler down, opened it, and the bird just sat there! Lori and I were about 25 feet in front of Charlie. Charlie then turned the cooler on its side and gradually eased the bird forward. When his talons hit the grass, he took off running, flapping his wings, gained altitude and flew up toward the trees! It was an awesome sight! He then circled us before he flew away, flapping his wing. I will always believe he was thanking us for saving him! He had a story to tell all his friends and they talked all night! Have you ever tried to sleep with a group of owls carrying on a loud conversation just outside your bedroom door?

I have lived with these wonderful creatures for more than 40 years! Never a day passes without something interesting happening. It is like living in a paradise! I have learned from all these wonderful creatures: tenacity, patience, observance, forgiveness, love how to live together in harmony, respect each other's space, sharing and most of all, they have taught me to be thankful for what I have and the privilege of sharing.

Footnote: The wire over the chimney had rusted and the next day a new, stronger mesh cover was installed, made from a stronger metal and finished so it would not rust. I can thank Moss-Marlowe, a local company for that!

But the story doesn't end here! One day I was cleaning up around the swimming pool. I picked up a red ball, turned around to put it into a box of toys and saw a female skunk quietly eating from the cat's bowl! "Oh gee!" I said, "Oh gee, Pat!" What do you do now?" The skunk was between me and the gate! I thought a minute, sat down on the stoop of the pool house and waited until the skunk finished eating and left, then I could go into the house. When she finished, she waddled onto to the pool cover to get a drink from the water around the cover pump, drank a few sips, looked up and saw me. She appeared to think a minute, then slowly made her way toward where I was sitting. I thought, "Pat, old girl, you are in deep poop now! What are you going to do?"

She got within 3 feet of me, sat down and appeared to be thinking. After a few seconds, I said "Hi! My name is Pat! What's your name?" She just looked at me, made not a squeak of a sound. I then said, "How about I call you Skunky?" Again, no movement or sound. Then I said, "Skunky, do want to play ball?" I threw the ball about 3 feet away from me, she turned, looked at it, then back at me. Finally, she turned again, shuffled over to the ball, picked it up and brought it back! I threw it again and she did the same thing. After a few throws of the ball, each time further away, I threw it a longer distance and when she turned to go get it, I went around the other side of the pool and into the house. The little lady looked for me, then left, taking the ball with her. Now, nearly every afternoon, around 5:00 pm, Skunky came back, bringing her ball, we played and that has been going on for 2 years! Oh! I forgot to mention that Skunky has had at least two litters of babies and she did bring them to visit occasionally!

But this is not the end of the story! This past winter one beautiful black cat with white markings had a litter of four kittens:, three beautiful black and white, and one with a small amount of white, but mostly gray. The gentleman who was working in the yard one day found one of the kittens in the yard, the gray and white one, and her back legs were dangling from a spinal injury. I called my friend, Debbie Laux, who has a cat rescue program and she came to my home to pick up the kitten and take it to a veterinarian to see if anything could be done to help the little fellow. Before she left we decided to look around to see if there were more kittens in the litter. We walked around the area where the gray kitten was found to see if there were, and we found two more kittens, black and some white. Debbie took them to be fostered, but we had missed one. Several weeks later the mama cat brought her baby to the feeding bowls! She is now a full grown cat and beautiful. She lives outdoors with the other feral cats. She comes to me when I begin putting out the feeding dishes, will come to the bedroom, look around and then run back out to get her meal! One day I hope I can tame her enough to be spayed and adopted by a family. That must be soon!

I have learned many lessons from these wonderful creatures: Tenacity patience, observance, forgiveness, love, how to live together in harmony, respecting each other's space, sharing and most of all peace. They have all made my life interesting and meaningful. These are lessons I will never forget!

I know at my age it would be best of I sold this house and grounds around it, but would the new owners take care of the wild life? Would they enjoy the beauty of the forest, especially when the trees are backlit by the descending sun just before dark, the beauty of heavy snow covering every surface during an occasional winter storm and watching the wildlife that hang around most of the time? The wonder of living with so many wild creatures, the beauty of the landscape and misty mornings, all have created a Shangri-la for me. Who would not enjoy that? This is a problem and must be thoroughly considered since I won't always be here. This house and the woods(forest) need to be enjoyed by people who appreciate the space, privacy, the wonderful creatures, and hopefully would be willing to continue feeding my outdoor family when I am no longer here!

A CHANGE OF MIND

The last trip I made alone was to France, and it was difficult. My flight home was no fun since the plane was was completely full, the noise level was the worst I had ever encountered, the food was hardly palatable, and I was exhausted. I had been in Europe for three weeks and for the first time was lonely, even though I had visited friends. My visits with them were wonderful, and I was missing them, but for some reason it wasn't the same as it usually had been in the past. I was homesick for the first time in many years of traveling. When I arrived home, I set my suitcase on the floor in the kitchen, fixed a cup of tea, got two cookies out of the freezer, thawed them in the microwave, and sat down to relax a few minutes before I began unpacking and doing the laundry. After a few minutes I said to myself. "Self, you need to make a decision on whether to continue to be a world traveler or become a real artist."

After a few minutes of thinking it over. I got up, took the suitcase into the bedroom, opened it and dumped the dirty clothes out on the bed. I took the clothes into the laundry room, started the washing machine, and while the clothes washed, I took a shower, then finished the laundry, all the while thinking about the situation. When the laundry was finished, I had made the decision to travel no more and become a real artist. That same afternoon I put the suitcase in the car, drove into town and donated it to one of the charities. That was about 20 years ago and I have never regretted that decision.

It was a while after this that I received an invitation to exhibit my work in galleries in China, Japan, and Korea. If you read this book, you will learn that I did send work to those countries, never made it to China but did go to Japan and Korea. Other than those trips, I have remained at home and sent paintings to galleries, made day trips now and then, but never had another extended voyage anywhere and don't plan on another one any time soon.

It has been wonderful getting reacquainted with local friends, making new ones, getting active in our fantastic local museum, having exhibitions closer to home, and spending time in my studio and now I am writing this book. I will admit, though, that lately I have been thinking about my friends in far-flung places. I have not been diligent in keeping up with them the way I should, and they have been quiet also. So, I have made a promise to myself to try to get in touch with them, catch up with their family happenings, and let them know how things are with me. I will try to be a better friend to them and my local contacts. Wish me luck. Who knows? Maybe I will be on a plane going somewhere before long, but don't bet on it.

AFTERWORD

My first experience with Pat Viles was when she had her solo exhibition at the Hickory Museum of Art. I was fairly new to my position at the museum and assisting with the intake of such a prolific, talented artist and her high caliber artwork intimidated me so. But it was during that intake that I discovered not only the beauty of her artwork but also of her soul. Pat is a generous, colorful, and kind person who reveals her beauty through each encounter she has with people and every time she touches a canvas. Her talent is beyond compare. Through workshops and classes, she has shared her methods, experiences, and travel, with the community and, in turn, has become an inspiration to all those around her. She layers her art with experience and wisdom in a way that leaves the viewer longing for more. Pat has invested herself in each piece as she does in each relationship. I feel honored to not only work in a museum which has collected her work but also to call her my dear friend. We, as a community, are better because of Pat, and the gift she has given us in her stories and artwork is a privilege we can enjoy for years to come. Not to mention her baking... Her shared talents are a beautiful treasure appreciated by all who are honored to know her. Especially me.

--Clarissa Starnes, Executive Director, Hickory Museum of Art

Made in the USA
Monee, IL
23 July 2023